Siblings and Autism

of related interest

Siblings
The Autism Spectrum Through Our Eyes
Edited by Jane Johnson and Anne Van Rensselaer
ISBN 978 1 84905 829 2

Families of Adults with Autism
Stories and Advice for the Next Generation
Edited by Jane Johnson and Anne Van Rensselaer
ISBN 978 1 84310 885 6

Voices from the Spectrum
Parents, Grandparents, Siblings, People with Autism, and Professionals
Share Their Wisdom
Edited by Cindy N. Ariel and Robert A. Naseef
ISBN 978 1 84310 786 6

At Home in the Land of Oz
Autism, My Sister, and Me
2nd edition
Anne Clinard Barnhill
ISBN 978 1 84310 859 7

Siblings and Autism

Stories Spanning Generations and Cultures

Edited by Debra Cumberland and Bruce Mills

Jessica Kingsley *Publishers*
London and Philadelphia

A version of "Visiting Becky" by Anne Clinard Barnhill was originally published in *At Home in the Land of Oz: Autism, My Sister, and Me*, Jessica Kingsley Publishers, 2007.

Debra Cumberland's "Sirens" originally appeared in *Under the Sun 12* (Summer 2007): 8–18.

Parts of Katie Harrington Stricklin's "On the Way to the Sky" appeared in "Doug's Aria: A Sister's Note on Autism," published in *Spectrum: For the Autism and Developmentally Disabled Community*, April/May 2010, and is published with permission of Spectrum Publications (spectrumpublications.com).

Excerpts from William Faulkner's *The Sound and the Fury* contained in Erica Nanes's "Family Reasemblance" come from the Vintage (Division of Random House) publication of the novel, and are reproduced with permission.

First published in 2011
by Jessica Kingsley Publishers
116 Pentonville Road
London N1 9JB, UK
and
400 Market Street, Suite 400
Philadelphia, PA 19106, USA

www.jkp.com

Library of Congress Cataloging in Publication Data
Siblings and autism : stories spanning generations and cultures / edited by Bruce Mills and Debra Cumberland.
    p. cm.
  ISBN 978-1-84905-831-5 (alk. paper)
  1. Autistic children--Family relationships. 2. Autism--Patients--Family relationships. 3. Brothers and sisters. I. Mills, Bruce, 1958- II. Cumberland, Debra.
  RJ506.A9S5266 2011
  618.92'85882--dc22
                              2010019256

British Library Cataloguing in Publication Data
A CIP catalogue record for this book is available from the British Library

ISBN 978 1 84905 831 5

Printed and bound in the United States by
Thomson-Shore, Inc.

Debra Cumberland
For my parents and for my brother

Bruce Mills
For Sarah Holtapp Mills

Contents

Acknowledgments

Debra Cumberland

Winona State University provided me with a sabbatical, which proved instrumental in allowing me the time to finish the project. I would like to thank my department chair Ruth Forsythe and my colleagues for their support. I would particularly like to acknowledge the assistance of Linda Kukowski and Kimberly Vogt.

Bruce Mills

I would like to thank Kalamazoo College for the sabbatical that, in part, contributed the time to develop the project and for the developmental money to advertise the call for essays. I am also indebted to those individuals who have graduated from or are currently attending Kalamazoo College, siblings who have shared their stories about life with a family member on the autism spectrum or with other physical or developmental disabilities: Sarah Bretz, Michael Tressler, Laura Mannion, Elizabeth Davis, Carolyn DeWitt, Claire Madill, Catherine Stover, Emily Bair, and Maddie Gillentine. Though it is hard to single out any one of the many wonderful students, I wish to thank Lindsey Fisch for initiating an independent study on sibling narratives and the joint learning that emerged from it. Finally, I am grateful for the help of colleague Dr. Babli Sinha who provided a contact for the Autism Society of India.

Deb and I both trace our investment in this project to the fall 2005 conference "Autism and Representation: Writing, Cognition, Disability," sponsored by the Society for Critical Exchange and organized, with the help of many certainly, through the tireless efforts of Mark Osteen. For the many who attended, this conference brought forth and produced an "empathetic scholarship" that has led to enduring professional connections, personal friendships, and essential scholarship. In addition, we would like to thank Sandra L. Harris, Donald Meyer, and Vicki Forman, who, at early stages in this project, provided helpful advice and/or assistance in circulating the call for essays.

And, of course, we are indebted to Rachel Menzies and Victoria Peters at Jessica Kingsley Publishers for their helpful editorial assistance and for Jessica Kingsley's commitment to this project and the many other publications doing such good work in and for the autism community.

Introduction

Debra Cumberland and Bruce Mills

Debra

As a young girl growing up in Storm Lake, Iowa, I was struck by how isolated my family felt with respect to my brother. We seemed to be the only family in the world who had a child with autism. The books on my parents' shelves, however, seemed to belie this fact—we had the *Noah* books (including Josh Greenfeld's *A Child Called Noah* and *A Place for Noah*), James Copeland's *For the Love of Ann*, and Barry Kaufman's *Son-Rise*, as well as other, more clinical, texts. Once we even watched a *60 Minutes* episode on autism, so I vaguely realized that there must be other people out there like my brother and that I could not be the only girl who had a sibling with autism. But it certainly felt as if I were alone, living in a small town in the 1970s. Sometimes people said, when I mentioned that I had a brother who was autistic, "Oh, what does he paint?" It would not be the first time that I encountered such confusion over the "autism" classification.

Classifying my brother also led to problems at school, where, here too, he did not fit in. At home, listening to my parents, I sensed their struggle to keep Adam in a regular public school classroom. We went to family therapy sessions in Cherokee, Iowa, which I hated, for I could intuit, even at a young age, that the psychiatrists there blamed my brother's autism on my mother. I, however, knew how much she loved him, knew that they were wrong, and could appreciate, every day, my parents' sacrifices to keep the family humming along.

Until I went to a summer writing program at Carleton College in Minnesota as a high school student and made a dear friend who also had a brother with autism, I did not recognize what a dramatic difference it made to have someone to talk with, to understand the unique dynamic facing a sibling relationship with a brother or sister with autism—or any other neurological or mental challenge. Prior to meeting this friend, I had felt that no one else had ever had this experience. Now, so many decades later, I have become increasingly struck by how hard it would be *not* to be aware of autism. Just driving down the streets of the town I live in, I regularly see billboards proclaiming how often a child is born with autism—now one in 150, according to a 2007 study by the United States Centers for Disease Control and Prevention— or notice advertisements for autism spectrum disorder groups on the cable access channel or in the paper. Everyone I meet seems to have heard of the disorder, although his or her information may not always be accurate. There has been an explosion of parent memoirs, the most famous right now being Jenny McCarthy's *Louder Than Words: A Mother's Journey in Healing Autism* (McCarthy 2007). Mark Haddon's novel *The Curious Incident of the Dog in the Night-Time*, with its first-person narrator who has autism, became an international bestseller. There are websites, such as Pray for Autism Now (P.A.N.)[1] and Neurodiversity.com. Everyone, it seems, has something to say about autism. But what are these blogs, memoirs, essays, and websites saying? What are the tales being told? And whose are the stories being heard?

or symbolic play.) Significantly, an autism diagnosis arises from close observation of behaviors, not from any blood analysis or, at least currently, from genetic testing. However, with a range of educational and therapeutic interventions, the more debilitating effects of autism can be somewhat alleviated, although it is a life-long disorder.

As demonstrated in a number of essays in this book, a part of the history of autism is the legacy of institutionalization. From the 1950s to the 1970s, prior to the deinstitutionalization that transformed care for many on the spectrum, one prominent option was to send the family member away. With relatively limited information about autism, parents and siblings often found themselves confronting behaviors that endangered the person with autism or, if not putting the child or others at risk, led to profound family disruptions. As painfully rendered in the essays of Anne Barnhill, Erika Giles, Maureen McDonnell, and Alison Wilde, families often sent their son or daughter, brother or sister, to the place that offered trained care providers, the potential for addressing difficult behaviors, and the promise of care unavailable within the limited resources of an individual household. Though families certainly sought to keep their son or daughter at home, it was part of the treatment plan to consider such institutional placements, a model that ran its course, for the most part, until the philosophical shift toward services based in communities (such as group homes) that led to extensive shutting down of psychiatric hospitals.

During this period, a central figure emerged in the story of autism: Bruno Bettelheim. As Debra Cumberland, Thomas Caramagno, and Matthew Belmonte directly address in this book, we still live in the shadow of his theories and practices concerning autism. A self-proclaimed expert on child development who frequently appeared on television, radio, and magazine covers, Bettelheim is most famously known for founding the Orthogenic School in Chicago and for his infamous book, *The Empty Fortress: Infantile Autism and the Birth of Self*, first published in 1967, which has forever influenced how we understand autism. In his book, he described a person living with autism as an "empty fortress" and argued the devastating position that autism is caused not just by bad parenting but by parents who did not wish their child existed. While he did not coin the term "refrigerator mother"—Kanner did, in 1943—he popularized the theory that autism was caused by the infant's relationship with his or her cold, intellectual, and unloving mother and that the autistic child built up barriers as a defense against abusive parenting. Framed in emotionally stirring language and compelling metaphors comparing children to Holocaust survivors and their parents to Nazi concentration guards, the ideas from *The Empty Fortress* seized the popular and professional imagination and still linger today. Kanner himself, who laid the foundation for parent blaming, later recanted his assertion of parents as the cause of autism at a meeting of the National Society for Autistic Children in 1968, but by then the damage was already done, embedded in the public narrative. And Bettelheim's persuasive metaphors continue to inform our understanding of the person with autism: the idea of individuals as nonhuman, cyborgs, computers, as people with a hidden or "normal" self waiting to break through. Through its title, Clara Claiborne Park's *The Siege: The First Eight Years of an Autistic Child*, a landmark parent memoir published in the same year as Bettelheim's book, indirectly (and unintentionally) acknowledges this dominate metaphor of breaking down the wall of autism— even as Park herself refused to accept Bettelheim's premises. So many stories, then, had to battle the master narrative promoted in *The Empty Fortress*.

We have traveled some distance from these years when autism was first dramatically entering public awareness. In an article in *Literature and Medicine*, Stuart Murray writes that autism "currently occupies a place in the public consciousness that is akin to a phenomenon," adding that the "increased rate of diagnosis (from one in several thousand in the 1970s to one in one hundred and fifty-eight today) has suggested to some that we live in an 'autism epidemic'" (Murray 2006, p.25). And the word *epidemic* is a powerful concept, inciting a sense of fear and calling up associations with plagues that sweep through the streets, something contagious, borne in the air or even ingested in food (Grinker 2007, p.5). Murray observes that, in the United States, the publication of David Kirby's *Evidence of Harm: Mercury in Vaccines and the Autism Epidemic: A Medical Controversy* (2005) ignited the intense debate over the causes of autism, while in the United Kingdom the possible dangers of the measles, mumps, and rubella (MMR) vaccine and its suggested link to autism created something of a media sensation.

In recent years (in part due to the capacity for computer technology to facilitate communication), we have a rich array of self-reporting from those on the spectrum—in books, on blogs, and during conferences and other public forums. In other words, we have a more expansive view of the internal world of autism, from Temple Grandin's works *Emergence, Animals in Translation,* and other books, to Daniel Tammet's *Born on a Blue Day* to Kamran Nazeer's *Send in the Idiots: Stories from the Other Side of Autism* to CNN's documentary of Sue Rubin in *Autism Is a World* to the blogs of Amanda Baggs and the widely accessed site, the Autism Hub. For the broader public as well as parents and siblings, autism is being reframed and redefined by those who had been previously silenced as well, a silence that came in part from narrow conceptions of personhood and limited notions of what constitutes communication. In short, a belief that autism represents different neurological wiring and thus a different way of processing and knowing the world is displacing views of autism as a kind of pathology. This "neurodiversity" perspective has already begun to orient people differently toward those with autism and will continue to inform and challenge how "neurotypicals"—that is, those off (or perhaps at a different place on) the autism spectrum—develop their own understandings and representations of a son or daughter, brother or sister, client or patient.

The essays within this collection must be understood within these definitions and histories. To know that Bettelheim asserted his direct or indirect presence on a family story is to gain insight into the plotlines that affect a sibling relationship. To know that institutionalization was a primary intervention is to understand that trauma or guilt might be a thematic legacy in a life and story. And to see that autism manifests itself along a broad spectrum, that some individuals may be nonverbal and others verbal, that some individuals must contend with profound sensory and social challenges, that others may have the ability (and supports) to engage in school and the workplace—all these differences along the spectrum affect the particular private and public dynamic for siblings.

Memoir and autism

Bettelheim's legacy and the current assertions of the importance of early intervention point to a continuing issue for both parents and siblings who write of their experiences. If their family member does not "recover" from autism—if indeed such a thing is possible—they may feel they have somehow failed and are somehow to blame for the individual's problems. They did not love enough; they did not try hard enough. Such a belief echoes Jenny McCarthy's "warrior mom" terminology evoked in *Louder Than Words* (McCarthy 2007), the popular, *New York Times* bestselling memoir of her son Evan and his "recovery" from autism, and later used as the title of her book that shares "recovery stories from parents across the country," according to Amazon.com. Bettelheim's contention that autism was caused by mothers who could not love, and therefore who created children who could not love, takes on a new twist today with websites such as Pray for Autism Now, which urges readers to embrace prayer as a way to heal their child from autism. McCarthy's memoir can be seen, in part, as an indirect response to Bettelheim's legacy because she attests that, if only mothers try hard enough, they can cure their child—and God will be on their side. As McCarthy writes, "[i]nstead of getting mad at God, like I'm sure a lot of people do, I decided to make him my buddy in this. I remember saying to Him around this time, 'God, I know you gave me my autistic son for a reason.'" She concludes that, "when you make God your buddy, He answers fast" (McCarthy 2007, p. 90). Along with this call to faith is an assertion of personal will, an affirmation of her individual resolve: "It was my dedication to asking questions and researching…that led us down the road to recovery." Though perhaps intended to provide an avenue of strength in times of despair, the spiritual rhetoric, unfortunately, implies that the parent has failed because he or she did not take the child's autism to God. Autism becomes a curse inflicted on the child because of a parent's personal failing—inadequate research, inadequate dedication, inadequate faith. For the sibling, for the brothers and sisters who accept or feel the pressure to take on the parental role, this urgent appeal to "cure" or "save" can produce a second generation of felt inadequacy.

The culture of blame, then, continues in a new form in the twenty-first century. And in the explosion of memoirs written about or by people with autism, many books utilize what Mark Osteen, the organizer of the 2005 Autism and Representation Conference, calls "the conversion narrative." (In the book that emerged from the work of the conference, *Autism and Representation* (Fisher 2007), James Fisher astutely tracks the tradition of this dominant plotting in his essay "No Search, No Subject? Autism and the American Conversion Narrative.") That is, many books about autism and most memoirs and personal essays are stories of recovery. As Osteen (and Fisher) noted at the conference, Americans especially love these types of stories because they conform to a cultural ideology of self-renewal, self-help, and pull-yourself-up-by-your-bootstraps-even-if-you-have-no-boots ethos. In this manner, parent and sibling blaming has taken on a new, perhaps more insidious form—another reason that we need to hear other stories, other narratives, in order to counteract this "salvation" and "conversion" understanding of autism. With a wider survey of stories, we can begin to see individuals with autism in a more complex, more human way, rather than as trapped individuals; as objects to be transformed, not subjects to be understood; as people with superhuman, living Google powers; as martyrs; or as somehow spiritually enlightened beings that will make others better people.

While often rooted in real evidence of praiseworthy and remarkable lives, these salvation, sacrifice, or savant representations of the autism story foster unrealistic expectations that may lead to anger, blame, and shame. In their poignant reflections on living with a sibling who has autism, in fact, some essays here point to the anger that can come from such unexamined, unforgiving expectations. In representing the sibling story as fraught with multiple (and often conflicting emotions), many of these writers seek to capture the un-Hollywood moments when loss and joy, resentment and responsibility, guilt and the desire for forgiveness coexist: the participation in a brother's dialogue on utility workers and bald men, the willingness to see the distinct features of a Thanksgiving card on a refrigerator, the release that comes from rocking out to The Clash's "Rock the Casbah" on the radio. In other words, the sibling story can provide a kind of counternarrative because such a perspective may arise from experiences askew from the parental lens or at odds with it—even as such stories convey the pressure to accommodate the demands of parenting alongside the poignant desire for a sibling bond.

Sibling stories

Over the past ten years, some publications have integrated sibling stories or sought to address the experience in relation to a "special needs" brother or sister, including Kate Strohm's *Being the Other One: Growing Up with a Brother or Sister Who Has Special Needs*, Bryna Siegel and Stuart Silverstein's *What about Me? Growing Up with a Developmentally Disabled Sibling*, Jeanne Safer's *The Normal One: Life with a Difficult or Damaged Sibling*, and Don Meyer's anthology *Thicker Than Water: Essays by Adult Siblings of People with Disabilities*. Focusing specifically on autism, *Siblings of Children with Autism: A Guide for Families* by Sandra L. Harris and Beth A. Glasberg and *Sibling Stories: Reflections on Life with a Brother or Sister on the Autism Spectrum* by Lynne Stern Feiges and Mary

Jane Weiss can be read as companion texts: a "study" based on interviews with a range of siblings and a book of brief, first-person narratives and interviews. It is important to note, however, that parent narratives dominate the memoir market and that the mental health field has tended to equate family with mothers (not fathers or siblings)—though the field of "sib" studies appears to be growing.

In the sibling literature addressing autism, however, three complete, stand-alone memoirs are especially compelling: Judy and Paul Karisik's *The Ride Together*, Anne Clinard Barnhill's *At Home in the Land of Oz: Autism, My Sister, and Me*, and Karl Taro Greenfeld's *Boy Alone: A Brother's Memoir*. These narratives defy the tendency to construct simple tales of recovery or redemptive self-sacrifice. Through essay and comic strip chapters, the Karisiks trace the relationship with their brother David from the 1950s to 2001, capturing their childhood resentments, their ongoing effort to develop meaningful bonds, and, ultimately, the need to answer a central family question, "What are they to do with David after their mother dies?" The unconventional book ends with an accommodation for David's life that discounts neither his core self and interests nor Judy's and Paul's poignant looking on. In *At Home in the Land of Oz*, Barnhill provides a perspective often missing, given the higher prevalence of autism among males: a sister-sister relationship. Six years older than Becky, Anne Barnhill conveys the impact of her sister's institutionalization (captured in her essay in this book) and the moving experiences of negotiating her own adolescence amid her sister's behaviors. Greenfeld's memoir—a brutally honest account of the rage, confusion, and love that he felt growing up in the shadow of Noah—is perhaps the most affecting when he constructs a section that imagines life with a "recovered" brother. Given the desire to "cure" or "recover" the person on the spectrum that often shapes the family (and autism) story, this aspect of the book invites readers to consider just how powerful such imaginings can be for the other child, the sibling who, often, has created so many tales of what cannot be alongside what is.

The lives represented in this anthology—those of the siblings —put further flesh on the bones of these narratives. Descendents of multiple cultural heritages, generations, classes, and ethnicities, the writers filter their memories and circumstances through different voices, lifestyles, and temperaments; in doing so, they draw from close study of and research on autism and, on occasion, the knowledge that comes only from years of observations. In our effort to gather essays, we sought writers within the United States and beyond, advertising in the publications of writing organizations, sibling networks, and autism agencies from around the world. Helen McCabe and Chuan Wu's "Our Family Has Two Hearts," Aparna Das's "Life with Runi," and Alison Wilde's "Sisters Aren't Doing It for Themselves" represent a start at placing the experience of autism within a cultural context. In China, for instance, autism was not diagnosed until 1982, according to McCabe and Wu, and there remains the understanding that the condition is a legacy for some type of family wrongdoing. (Such a view cannot help but recall the enduring influence of Bettelheim's theories in the United States.) In reflecting on efforts to find a place for her sister, Das calls attention to expectations concerning family obligations (and living arrangements) that suggest cultural values less resonant with, for instance, an American emphasis on leaving home and setting up an independent, more nuclear, and less extended family. Writing of her experience in England, Wilde critiques this individualistic ethos toward addressing disability, drawing attention to the social and institutional dynamics that isolated her and her family and continue to affect parents and siblings. In its reflection on experiences spanning the United States, England, and India, Matthew Belmonte's "Autism Connects Us" also invites readers to see autism through a cultural lens. And, as we have noted earlier, we can observe writers from the cultural milieu of the United States directly and indirectly speaking to the historical legacy of Bettelheim and the conversion and recovery paradigms of McCarthy.

Though capturing the different ways in which brothers and sisters have experienced and represented their story, however, we also see the points of contact that create connections across cultures, generations, family dynamics, and ranges of impairment. Throughout various essays in this collection, for instance, writers worry that their family situation is something they caused—or that there is a need, somehow, for them to make up for some absence or lack. Thomas Caramagno movingly tells of his quest to compensate by being a great intellect, to "earn recognition, even love, through overachievement," a desire echoed by Maureen McDonnell, who writes, "I have spent my life passing, trying to prove that genetics are a fluke, that my parents aren't incapable of raising children. My stubbornness helped me fulfill the trappings of the successful child." Belmonte offers another variation on this theme; he tells of sabotaging the role of "trophy" child that, in his experience, arose from his father's inability to reconcile his dreams of an idealized family life with the fact of his oldest son's autism.

The urge to prevail over real and perceived troubles comes with its own trappings of guilt as well as the often-present accompanying silence—how to explain the family narrative, particularly in a time when so little was known and the very little that was known was so clearly ill-informed. Many of these essayists, including Caramagno, were fortunate to have parents who were very much involved in trying to understand, and overturn, those harmful narratives. However, one option, for many families, was and has been not to explain it at all but to maintain a culture of silence in the face of so much misinformation and potential rejection. Katie Harrington Stricklin movingly recounts how her family maintained this silence outside their circle. Moreover, she writes that friends did not ask about her brother's behaviors and that she did not offer an explanation, confessing "I had this gut feeling that if the word [autism] were out in the open, it would have been used to hurt Doug even more."

In addition to this desire to compensate for a brother or sister who is not "normal," the writers capture the feeling that there, too, must be something "wrong" with them. Catherine Anderson gestures toward the specter of "becoming the other," while Anne

Barnhill "wondered if something in me might go crazy." Because, in many of these essays, there was a time when the sibling seemed "normal," the child's fear that the situation can change overnight especially burdens the early years. And if not concerned with succumbing to "illness" or some hidden disease, writers sometimes wonder if they too might be sent away, just as their brother or sister was taken to another place and seemingly abandoned.

The narratives also recall youthful moments when anger and guilt arise from observing and confronting hypocrisy in others and oneself. In "Victim of Silence," Ann Damiano depicts how her Catholic school classmates taunt her brother as a "retard" but, during a lesson on tolerance to minorities, one nun will not provide support when she calls out her peers on their behavior. Her story is the more poignant because she, too, has at times rejected her own brother for his behaviors. (Perhaps we can see current work within disability rights and the effort to end use of the "r" word as finally taking to heart the full implications of Damiano's experiences.) Mental disabilities are often the ones that are the least understood and therefore the most feared; thus, they bring out latent prejudices that siblings must confront in the society around them and, painfully, within themselves. To balance righteous anger or the pride of taking a stand with the private shame of rejecting a brother or sister with autism is a heavy burden. Here, then, is one telling feature of the sibling story: the inner turmoil that comes from seeing oneself in the cruel actions of others, from feeling the anger directed outward rebound upon oneself in guilt and self-blame.

At their most poignant, sibling stories recount or confront the long-term implications of a family tie to autism. Sometimes directly addressed but most often implied is the decision to remain close to a brother or sister and so to have the chance to meet and share communication that cannot be done from a distance. Such moments come forward in many of the essays. We see, then, how to live out and write of the obligation of caring for someone with a disability and the struggles and complications involved in honoring that commitment, particularly with the realization that this reality shall, in all likelihood, remain constant. Perhaps a simple but often unrecognized truth, one that may not find its way into the many other narratives on autism, is that siblings will most likely live the longest time with the family member on the spectrum. They are the ones who will see a brother or sister age; they will have the burden of the storyteller who alone can unlock the past with a shared memory.

But there is another dimension of this enduring blood connection. When dealing with the genetic component to autism, siblings must also consider the very real possibility that their own children will be on the spectrum. In "Family Resemblance," Erika Nanes confronts this issue when her friend has a baby diagnosed with Down syndrome and decides to have an abortion since "we wouldn't be very good parents to a child like that." Haunted by her friend's decision, Nanes nonetheless asks herself the same question: "If my only choice were a child with autism or none at all, what would I do? I don't want to ever imagine the question. But it hovers, unanswered, nonetheless." At their core, then, such stories ask the very real question of the nature of our obligations toward each other, as well as our obligations toward ourselves. Negotiating these responsibilities can be extraordinarily difficult. To give voice to them, to find a vocabulary for such negotiations, tests writers, often leading them to the stories of others. In her effort to articulate her own conflicted emotions, for instance, Nanes evokes William Faulkner's *The Sound and the Fury* and its depiction of a rebellious Caddy Compson and her mentally retarded young brother Benjy.

While many of the essays in this anthology do have a similar trajectory—identifying difference and the struggle to acknowledge, accept, and understand that difference—they also reveal most tellingly the tremendous strides that we have made in understanding autism, as well as the distance we have yet to travel. Stories such as those by Erika Reich Giles and Cara Murphy Watkins are among the many that focus on the lack of knowledge regarding autism in the 1950s through 1970s, when next to no one knew anything about the disorder. For Giles's brother, such a diagnosis meant a life in an institution. The annual journey visiting her brother, as well as the accompanying feelings of remorse and guilt, are heart wrenchingly evoked in Giles's "Robie." In "His Little Sister," a story that reflects a more understanding environment (at least in her own neighborhood), Watkins still observes that most people had "never heard of the term" *autism*. Quite likely, the humor that Watkins brings to her remembrances is hard won, the outcome of traveling her community with her brother without any shared vocabulary to explain his fascination with strangers' bald heads. Lindsey Fisch's piece, however, shows how much more knowledge and understanding people have of the condition today. In her writing, Fisch tells of calling 9-1-1 to seek help in rescuing her brother from his entrapment in the laundry chute; when she says, "He's autistic," she can, amazingly, count on the fact that the volunteer will know what she means.

* * *

Personal stories can represent, and help us understand, these complex human ties and tensions in a way that clinical studies cannot. For one thing, such writing can be the means of reaching beyond potentially stigmatizing clinical language by conveying lived experiences in vivid ways. The personal essay reveals that, though stories may share common plotlines, the *individual* voice has its own inflections and lyrical power, as demonstrated by Debra Eder's compression of time and memories in "My Brother's Speaker." In the end, stories give us a human face to challenges and joys that too often remain faceless.

Art is empathy. And for us, the editors of this anthology, an empathetic art serves the storytellers and their communities. While the goal of this volume is to collect the work by siblings and to foster empathy and understanding, it also aims to recognize these writers' valuable contributions to literature as a whole—to underline connections rather than focus on differences. In short, these essays consistently demonstrate the desire to connect, to understand our common humanity, and to find one's place among others.

While there is great value in critiquing our understanding of what is "normal" and in seeing the contributions of those who are neurologically atypical, it is also important to realize that doing so does not—and cannot—eradicate the challenges of those with neurological disorders or different ways of knowing, however we choose to speak of it. Reading and reflecting on well-told stories, however, can illuminate how part of our problem lies in consistently thinking of ourselves in isolation from others. Our common work, then, resists this isolating impulse; it's the ongoing labor of living with and sharing our different ways of knowing in the world. To live together in this space, after all, we need to hear and to honor the stories that come of these efforts, all of them.

Notes

1. Pray for Autism Now. Available at http://sites.google.com/site/ autismhome/Home/god-s-intervention/pray-for-autism-now.

References

Grinker, R.R. (2007) *Unstrange Minds: Remapping the World of Autism.* New York: Basic Books.

Murray, S. (2006) "Autism and the Contemporary Sentimental: Fiction and the Narrative Fascination of the Present." *Literature and Medicine 25*, 1, 24–45.

McCarthy, J. (2008) *Louder Than Words: A Mother's Journey into Healing Autism.* New York: Plume.

House on the Meadow

1

Catherine Anderson

I am the sister of an autistic man, my almost-twin, my stranger. We share the memory of a house we lived in together as children over forty years ago, a small house with a yard as large and verdant as a meadow. Like the writer Jules Michelet's description of how a bird creates the circle of a nest by pressing the walls round and round with its body, my brother Charlie and I sang our songs, played our games, pressed our circle of twigs and mud until the nest became a home. Then quite suddenly, my brother had to leave us for a cinder-block institution where he slept on a rail bed for eight years in a room shut from all dreams.

In the early seventies when my brother Charlie was seventeen, the institution in Michigan where he lived was closed down. Eventually, my parents found a group home and a sheltered workshop for him near us in Kansas City, Missouri. Now a tall, husky man of fifty-three, he earns approximately $25 per month and signs his paycheck by meticulously printing each letter of his name in large, block letters. For years, when both my parents were alive, he liked to attend St. Mary's Episcopal Church with them, dressing up in a suit and tie, taking a ride downtown, entering through large wooden doors to be greeted by warm, church-going faces. Though he is severely disabled, with profound speech impairments, he would try to return every greeting with a quick, chirpy hello. Later, at coffee hour, he would forego conversation and head straight for the brightly iced cookies. These days he enjoys bowling with his group-home roommates and attending weekend dances sponsored by the city's Parks and Recreation Department. For an autistic individual with minimal speech, my brother does well in an otherwise dog-eat-dog world simply because his attention is narrowed to the most essential: the names of his relatives and his roommates, the food he likes, and the colors that delight him. What more does a person need?

A few summers ago I lived alone in a small house by a meadow, set in the foothills of Mount Monadnock in central New Hampshire. I came to this house for the same reason anyone takes off alone—to quiet the mind's rough, internal noise. Pine branches brushed the sides of the house, lavender edged the door. Looking out a window at the florid meadow and beyond, I would enter again and again the mountain's blue shadow. Up at the cabin for a few weeks, my life, like my brother's, would be pared down to a few simple things: my watercolor paints, pens and notebooks, wood for the fire, coffee for breakfast. The jutting gables and lean lines of the old cabin suggested, in the slightest of terms, the house of our childhood. I trusted that this spareness would help me learn what I could by looking more deeply at nature, finally settling down long enough to turn over those questions that had always obsessed me: Who is Charlie deep inside? What are his inner thoughts? How does he imagine, and what does he dream?

One morning, Mount Monadnock was a blue-gray curtain in the distance, while up close, the meadow was filled with brilliant-colored wild flowers, all with ordinary names—yarrow, ox-eyed daisy, bluebells, clover. Not a large meadow, but what a world! It occurred to me that entering my brother's mind must be like taking a long, zigzagging walk into the country. As humans in nature, we have to honor other animals and their living spaces: we're only visitors. We have to walk slowly and listen intently, focusing on sounds, smells, and motion. The trick is to get comfortable with these nonsymbolic impressions and reach beyond the self, with the intuition of art. So it is with my brother Charlie—complete attention to all surrounding stimuli, with no map or guidebook for direction. I must attend not only to *what* he thinks but also to *how* his mind takes in the sensory details of sound and color and to how he, in return, expresses what he thinks and feels: a smile, the focus or muttering of a single word that at first seems indecipherable.

My parents had been mystified by Charlie's behavior since he was a cranky one-and-half-year-old, fascinated by spinning objects but not imitating speech of any kind. The word *autistic* was never used to describe my brother because the diagnosis had not yet reached mainstream recognition. Instead, he was "diagnosed" alternately as "mentally retarded" and "mentally ill." This combination disqualified him for special-education classes in the public schools, though he always did very well on any nonverbal intelligence test. Years later, my mother read about autism and questioned our family physician who agreed that his behaviors all matched the description; yet it was too late for Charlie to qualify for any special education. His diagnosis is still officially "organic brain syndrome," and after so many years, no one, including me, has ever sought to change it.

To this day, my brother and I communicate through lines of gesture and utterance and a vocabulary rooted to colors, flavors, old tunes, a language all its own. I learned this language from my mother, an accomplished speech therapist (or "correctionist" as the profession was called in the 1950s) when she realized that her retarded, mentally ill son would need years and years of coaching before uttering a single word. Like any child eager to please, I instinctively followed my mother's attempts to communicate with Charlie and soon was helping her decode his agitated hand-flapping and squeals when a noise disturbed him or his shirt was buttoned the wrong way. At other times, Charlie surprised us with masterful one-liners, a kind of haiku speech. Once, when he was ten or eleven and living at the institution, he came home to spend Christmas with us. In the 1950s and 1960s, my father was a newspaper reporter, and in between trips to Eastern Europe, he "worked midnights," as he put it, with no holidays or weekends off. Like many city reporters of the time, my father would stop off after work for a drink or two at the local tavern, not a habit my mother liked to encourage. Charlie must have sensed the tension, and he probably overheard an occasional argument between them. That particular Christmas, however, I am sure my father came home directly, with no stops at the Anchor Bar. But when he came through the door that night, Charlie greeted him with a giggly shout of "Rednose!" This continued for days, every time my father entered the room. We knew that Charlie loved the song "Rudolph the Red-nosed Reindeer," but if he was aiming for the guilty vein of my father's heart, he couldn't have been a better shot.

These one-line phrases flash suddenly out of the darkness like comets and disappear just as swiftly. "Nuts and bolts" was the answer Charlie, now an adult, gave my mother when she asked him (many times, perhaps for years) what he did at his sheltered workshop. We had no idea where he got that—the workshop was a strict paper-and-package kind of place. On a visit home a few years ago, I thought I could pick up the usual routine of prompting him to talk by asking question after question about what he had for lunch, who he drank soda with at work, the name of his group-home roommates, and such. He made a few curt, stuttering tries and then gave up, saying, "Shut up, Cathy." He blinked and cocked his head in triumph. I was thrilled.

* * *

Gold-sparked daisies, clusters of purple clover, the meadow reveals hundreds of hues, subtle and stunning, a journey opening out to infinity and all its promise. Then, as the clouds pass, the meadow is nothing again and what we see only quick and fading, like fact and its memory. The meadow is both beautiful and blank. My experience with Charlie, too, has this essence. I love my brother, yet all I know of him vanishes when I meet the calm loam of his silence. Because I can understand him with such intimacy, I accept the greater burden of our relationship; yet, I don't know what this will mean as he ages, becoming even more inarticulate and speechless. We are both growing older, and with our parents no longer alive, the question of responsibility glows anxiously, a low-flame heat.

As a culture, we haven't been successful in taking care of the silent creatures among us, even though we share an intimacy with them and delight in their beauties.

"The big brains aren't of much help these days," the naturalist John Hay once told a gathering of nature writers at the New England Aquarium. A huge man, then in his seventies, Hay started his talk by honoring the aquarium as the "great house of the fish." He didn't hide his disgust with the ruin our high-minded civilization has made of nature. We have neglected to empathize with intelligences other than our own, and the result is polluted, fished-out waters, species extinction, a legacy of waste, he claimed. We've also lost the joy of knowing a different kind of perception. Ordinary barn swallows, Hay explained, are unusually sensitive to the nuances of weather and the changing patterns of the stars. Their speed and alacrity are signs of their intelligence, their understanding of a unique world, distant from us. In watching these birds, Hay said, "You really feel you are missing out on something."

The angle of light through clouds, the flow of wind over land, the night tilt of the earth. I don't think it is possible to approximate the mind of a swallow, and I don't believe I will ever fully understand how my brother thinks. The best I can do is pose a metaphor, find a parallel in a natural world that may be described but never known.

As a child, my brother was a grass-eater, his lips smudged green whenever he returned from wandering our backyard filled with blue chicory, Queen Anne's lace, and stubborn nut grass. I once asked him, "Charlie, why did you eat all that grass when you were a kid?" Even though he understood the teasing in my voice, he could only repeat the question back to me in his lazy style of echolalia, a back-and-forth loop of mutters and monosyllables, a habit that has always bewildered my family. Over the years, Charlie has made slow progress at initiating speech, and with prompting, he can make a tentative request for water or respond to ordinary questions clearly and fully. But sometimes he is tired and regresses into the echolalic habits of his childhood. That's when we all feel defeated, as if he could slip away beyond all return.

I now believe he ate grass because to him it tasted good, along with the flower tops he popped into his mouth like candy.

Once, alone in the New Hampshire meadow, as the last rays of sunlight were slowly sifting through the trees toward dusk, I waited for the gray line of the mountain's slow return in the final, soft hours of the day. I settled in a lawn chair with a book and then heard, as if for the first time, the high call-and-response notes of the wood thrushes echoing through the trees. I lay back and listened, truly listened, for more than half an hour—each song folded into the next, riff on riff, light trills floating through the firs as the sun fell. And that was enough. I expected no more from those birds than their own sweet tunes.

So, my brother's halting, spiraling echoes, his half-answered words and broken utterances, a kind of speech.

The stories my family has told and retold of Charlie's encounters with nature are the resonant echoes of a mind we can never understand. Each one of us has a separate Charlie-in-nature story, unique and unwitnessed by any other member of the family. If I told my mother, father, or younger brother about my understanding of his echolalia, they would listen a bit, then spin their own vivid and idiosyncratic tales. My story would drift away, as stories do until another memory echoes once again, the story's powerful source, and carries it into speech. My mother told us once that she remembers Charlie waking up at dawn on summer mornings to run outside to our overflowing backyard. From the kitchen window, she would watch as Charlie walked through the yard, birds landing near his feet, chattering and squawking as he waved his hands and arms. I never saw Charlie with the birds, but I do remember how Sam, our long-legged, hardworking airedale terrier, would follow him outside, guarding his every move, ready to bark and gnaw at his shoes if he tried to climb the fence. After Sam was rewarded for his vigilance, the dog would run in wide circles through the yard, his head bent to the ground, hind legs angled low in the ritual chase of his bear-hunting ancestors. Charlie and I would stand in the middle of Sam's winding circles, watching his earnest, panting spirals as if we were cornered players in his wild and ancient game. The animal Charlie enjoys drawing most easily, using a slender felt-tipped pen on lined notebook paper, is an animated, round-pawed dog with roughly shaped ears, tongue, and stubby tail.

As children we lived in a subdivision built on the edge of farmland in southern Michigan, not far from an industrial pottery factory that blew its whistle on time at seven a.m, and again at eleven a.m., then all through the shifts. But also near our home was a large, wooded park by the Clinton River where my parents took us for picnics. On these trips, as we drove closer to the large, bending oaks and elms, my brother calmed his squeals and persistent kicking. My mother noted this change in his mood, and I started to pay attention, glimpsing a bit of his nature unknown in any other context. In those woods, another child emerged, with a keen sense of solitude, a deep attention to the play of wind on the river or the scent of pines above the ridge. He relaxed, smiled, even hummed a song he liked. In these scenes, I have a brother who is equal in intelligence and emotion to anything within his surroundings—not a "retarded child" but simply a kid, walking through white birches and ferns with his sister, brother, mother, and father.

Some of the stories my family tells of Charlie's fondness for nature may be apocryphal, but we have to repeat them, especially to people outside the family who ask us, "What is Charlie like? What does he do?" These stories are retold not only to elevate him in our eyes but also to explain his unusual soul and present him, in the best light, to the doubting world. Michael Berube, the father of a son with Down syndrome, calls this attitude "bragging rights" in his book, *Life As We Know It*. We must, for the sake of our loved one's survival, bring attention to these gifts, make note of his rare mode of perceiving, his unique expression. We must yell it out, draw big pictures, brag and boast. In this spirit, I wonder if my brother's unique take on the world, his orientation and understanding of himself and those around him, could be that of a highly sensitive and intuitive *animal*. I say this with full admiration: my brother's loneliness and burly physique make him a bear; his loyalty is that of the wolf; his appetite and earnestness belong to the dog, as his twirling, echoing speech places him beside the songbirds of his youth.

However often I rise to the occasion of defending my brother's difference, the rich animal soul buried inside him, the silent man who feels deeply, the more aware I am of his limits. As a growing child, I became very aware of the differences between us, sensing both my good luck not to be born autistic as well as that emotion's opposite—an eerie, almost throbbing guilt. I was the fortunate daughter. Who knows what would happen to my retarded brother? One Sunday morning, my father had cooked bacon and eggs for all of us. After a few bites, Charlie squealed, then slouched down to the floor and wiped his dirty hands on his head. My father asked me to finish up the food he had left on his plate. I refused vehemently, shouting that if I ever ate anything already tasted by him, I would instantly turn into "a Charlie." In a more striking dilemma, there lived near my home a girl who was my age, another Cathy who could have been a mirror to my life, if I had not been so lucky. She was overweight with bad skin, a perennial failing student who spoke in halting, half-formed sentences. She inspired the same twinned feelings of repulsion and protection my brother Charlie had so often triggered. Even though I should have known better, I reacted like a typical adolescent: welcoming one minute, then shunning her later in small, hurtful ways: not inviting her to sit at the lunch table with my friends or not returning her phone calls. Because I could at this time in my life, because no one demanded that I offer more than the slightest kindness to this lonely girl, I kept her at a distance. She was too frightening. She was the specter of what my future would be: an uneven relationship between me and a brother who couldn't speak, couldn't read, and would be powerless to protect himself.

Today many socializing forces still work to control my brother's life: a strict diet and twice-daily medication, the rules of the sheltered workshop and his group home. At the same time, these strategies stabilize his anxiety, make his adjustment and growth possible. This paradox was set in motion years ago. When he was a child in the mid-1960s, Charlie was told not to come back to grade school because, as my mother put it, "he kicked the kindergarten teacher." Eventually, my parents placed him in an institution, a training school at a former army base near Battle Creek, Michigan, three-and-a-half hours away and the only place that would provide the regimented education that eight-year-old Charlie, mentally retarded and mentally ill, could respond to. He lived with seventy other children on one ward. For eight years, he learned colors, numbers, letters, and the basics of washing and dressing himself—an education in tedium, but it was the education that saved him.

In an old photograph, our childhood house casts a long, dark wing over the yard. The shadow almost touches us, my mother reaching for a squirming baby—our younger brother—and Charlie, scooting farther and farther away. I am off to the side. We are all dressed in sweaters. I must be ten and Charlie eight at the time, weeks before he left for the institution. Every child's story should be a circle of flight and return, the promise of home. I wish that were my brother's story, instead of years and years of living in an institution. If I could, I would give him the homecoming he missed—a walk through a flowering understory of dogwoods and red cedars, out to the wild meadow, and back to the small house and its round, bird-pressed nest.

All relationships compel us to use the tools of an artist: color and exaggeration, patience and craft. Whenever my brother sees me, his face bursts into a wide, brilliant smile that he holds, in silence, for minutes. How his cheeks must ache! On my visit to the New Hampshire hills, I remember rushing to get there before sundown, then quickly pulling out my watercolors to paint the meadow grasses and mountain at rest. When I started to paint, Mount Monadnock was almost invisible, a blended mist hugging the earth. Then slowly, within minutes, the mountain returned, in waving shades of lavender, orange, and rose. Don't ask me how the meadow appeared: I couldn't catch it in time. Shadowed green patches? Swaths of gold and bronze? The hues were too transitory as the meadow faded into evening, so much like the relationships we carry for a lifetime. Because my brother can't put into words his dreams or desires or why, this time, he is so happy to see me, I color in quick bold strokes the space his silence leaves empty, the truest shape of his presence.

Family Resemblance

2

Erika Nanes

The phone rings at 6:30 a.m. "Erika? Are you there?" It's Ellie, sobbing into my answering machine. I roll over, pick up. "I've been up all night. The test was positive. The baby has Down's."

Somehow, I find a way to respond. Even as I say them, I know that the words are clichéd. But I am too afraid of saying the wrong thing to deviate from the acceptable phrases: I'm sorry. You must be devastated. Can I help?

* * *

I am supposed to visit my brother Bruce this coming week in the apartment he shares with his caregivers. Though he lives forty minutes away, I see him only every two or three months. Sometimes those visits consist of a quick trip to a McDonald's or Jack in the Box restaurant after I accompany him to a doctor's office. When I am doing the Good Sister calculus, I count those visits. When I am doing the Bad Sister calculus, I leave them out.

* * *

In my earliest memory, my brother and I are both dressed in sailor suits, sitting together in the back of the family car. The sky is gray and heavy, the air muggy and unmoving, as it always was on summer afternoons in the Maryland suburb where we lived then. I sit next to him, looking at the backs of our parents' heads, thinking: family. This is what family means. It means that I sit in a certain place in the car. That I am part of a unit of two, called children. That there will always be heads in the front seat, to drive, to steer. I do not remember feeling especially happy or safe at this moment. No, just defined, contained: this is my place in the world. I am a daughter. I am a sister.

* * *

Though I was a childhood bookworm, I never found a novel or story that described a family like mine. So it was a shock when, as an adult, I discovered William Faulkner's *The Sound and the Fury*. The novel turns on the relationship between Caddy Compson, the rebellious daughter of the Compson family, and Benjy, her retarded younger brother. Unlike the rest of the Compsons, Caddy cares deeply for Benjy, but her sexual awakening and its consequences estrange her from her family. In one of the book's final scenes, the servant Luster, frustrated because Benjy is crying, says, "You want something to beller about? ... Caddy! Beller now. Caddy! Caddy! Caddy!" Benjy, reminded of the sister he hasn't seen for years, collapses into an inconsolable blur of sobs. Reading the scene for the first time, I felt the muscles in my chest become tense with effort. *Don't feel it. Don't cry. Don't become helpless, like him.*

* * *

"So, when are you going to decide what to do about the baby?" I ask Ellie. It's 7:35 a.m. We've been on the phone for over an hour.

"I think we've already pretty much decided," she says. "I mean, we wouldn't be very good parents to a child like that."

A child like that. "That's right," I think, surprising myself. "You wouldn't be." (*Did I say that out loud?*)

"And, you know, I'm just not sure what his quality of life would be."

"Oh, my brother seems to do okay," I say, forcing my tone to remain light.

"Really? You think he's happy?"

Happy? That word hadn't occurred to me. I thought of a book by an autistic man named Birger Sellin—who, like Bruce, can barely speak—that I'd read the previous summer. Called *I Don't Want to Be Inside Me Anymore* (1996), it described the man's frustration at not being able to make his needs known. He would scream for hours, hit people near him, then return to his room and type furiously about how isolated he felt from the world. How no one would ever understand him. How he would never be able to make them understand him.

"Yes," I said. "I think he's happy. Maybe not in the way that you and I would think about it, but yes, I think he is."

I don't entirely believe the words, even as I say them. But I don't entirely disbelieve them, either. Besides, saying anything else feels disloyal. Like criticizing the home team to a visitor from another city who never thought they played well anyway.

* * *

When Bruce is agitated or angry, he bites his lower arm. "Ahhpp!" he shouts, before he sinks his teeth into the already irritated area between his wrist and his elbow. "Ahhmm!" His expression when he bites himself is a mixture of defiance and frustration, a not-so-silent "now will you shut up?" combined with a hint of "because I don't know what I'll end up doing if you don't." Sometimes when I visit him, his entire lower arm is crisscrossed with red bumps and welts, a map of everything that has happened to upset him over the last few weeks. A few times, he has kicked holes in his bedroom door. I think of that when I find myself dealing with voice-mail delays or rush-hour traffic by slamming things—my hand against the phonebook, my palms on the steering wheel, my car door.

* * *

I...we stopped in the hall and Caddy knelt and put her arms around me and her cold bright face against mine. She smelled like trees.
"You're not a poor baby. Are you. You've got your Caddy. Haven't you got your Caddy."

* * *

I met Ellie a few years ago. We were both graduate students living in one of southern California's suburban ghettoes, linked by our desire to escape into the interesting. On one of our first escapades together, she smuggled buffalo wings into a Smashing Pumpkins concert. That was classic Ellie: not bending the rules, just behaving according to what she thought they should be. Of course, I hadn't been willing to stuff the Styrofoam container into my bag. Always the rule-follower, the good girl, I was content to have her do it for me.

* * *

After people learn that my brother has autism, their faces take on a particular look. I realize that they are about to ask The Question. The Question can take one of two forms. In its positive form, it concerns special talents, as in, "So, can your brother count cards [play Bach from memory, solve differential equations on sight, pinpoint which day October 15 will fall on in 2045]?" These are the silver-lining people, the ones who believe in payoffs. Then there are the other ones. Like me, they expect the worst and take their bad news straight. They usually ask about Bruce's level of intelligence. Except that they don't use that word. They ask, "Does he, um, function normally?" Or, if they're feeling bold, "What is your relationship with him like, exactly? How well does he remember you when you're not there?"

I don't blame people for asking these questions. They are the same ones I ask myself after each visit.

* * *

My mother once told me that as an infant, I exhibited behavior similar to my brother's. I crouched in my crib, rocking it back and forth, for hours. I was a late talker, and when I finally began to speak, I treated syllables like worry beads, swishing them back and forth in my mouth before letting them escape, untested, into the air from which I could never snatch them back. That I once shied away from words, from speech, is hard to believe for anyone who knows me now. To this day, though, I find myself curling up slightly in moments of stress, wanting nothing more than to rock, gently, in the unending yes/no, open/close rhythms of the world.

* * *

A week after our early morning phone call, I drive up to visit Ellie, who is staying with her parents while she recuperates from the abortion. It's summer, so neither of us has papers to grade or lessons to plan; we can cook elaborate meals and talk late into the night. We toss spinach with red onions and oranges, slice avocados, slather freshly ground peanut butter on nubby brown bread. She jokes that she can't use the excuse of eating for two anymore. My mind flashes the words to make her feel better. So I say, "Well, pretty soon maybe the two of you can start to try again."

Her face darkens for a second. "People keep saying that," she says. "As if it helps. I mean, in a way, it just makes me feel worse."

"Why?"

"Well, because. It just reminds me of everything. And it means I have to deal with peoples' questions. Even if they aren't saying anything, they're wondering, "What happened?" She pauses. "The truth is, I had a baby. And I killed it."

Because it wasn't the right kind of baby, I think. (*Don't say that.*)

"You can't blame yourself for knowing your own limits," I say. "I know what it's like to be responsible for someone who's disabled."

"But you said you thought your brother had an okay quality of life."

"In some ways, he does. In a lot of ways. But it's a lot of work to make sure that's the case. And he'll never be able to take care of things himself."

I believe everything I am saying. One part of me understands my friend's decision all too well. I know what my parents endured: the years of doctors' offices and depleted bank accounts as they searched for a diagnosis, the sleepless nights spent wrangling over this school or that. Couples with disabled children consistently report more marital distress than couples without. Two of my married friends have children labeled developmentally delayed: one of the two couples has had counseling for years.

How could I disagree with her decision? Wouldn't I do the same thing? (*I would. I wouldn't. I don't know.*)

* * *

My brother's daily uniform, circa 1979: shorts, shirt, sneakers. A Polaroid camera around his neck. In his hands, two magnifying glasses and a thatch of just-snapped photos. People walking by him in the supermarket would stop and stare at the boy peering through a magnifying glass while rocking back and forth and muttering to himself. That year, I stopped listening only to the part of me that said *be patient, be polite, they don't know what's wrong.* I learned to glower back, unmoving, until they lowered their eyes.

* * *

In the late nineteenth century, the French psychologist Alfred Binet labeled developmentally disabled children *debile* or "weak." Later, the eugenicist Henry Goddard developed an alternative term: *moron*, from the Greek word for "stupid and foolish." The less offensive word *retarded* eventually replaced both. Now parents and bureaucrats call the disabled "special," and kids who want to insult each other say, "Nice one, dude. What are you, *special?*"

* * *

"Goodbye, Bruce!" I say, as I always do when I get ready to leave after visiting him. "Thank you for letting me come over." I've finally come by to take him out for a fast-food lunch and snap some photos before the school year starts and I have the ever-present excuse of student papers to hide behind.

He extends his right hand to me. I shake it. "Thank you! Now, can I have a hug?"

Carefully, looking over my left shoulder, he edges up to me with arms extended. I've read that personal contact is painful for autistic people, as it exacerbates the sensory overload that accompanies their condition. With that in mind, I hug him as if I were trying not to hug him. He still backs away as soon as possible. I tell myself that, secretly, he is pleased.

* * *

We went along the fence and came to the garden fence, where our shadows were. My shadow was higher than Luster's on the fence. We came to the broken place and went through it.

"Wait a minute." Luster said. "You snagged on that nail again. Can't you never crawl through here without snagging on that nail."

Caddy uncaught me and we crawled through.

* * *

45

On my refrigerator, I've taped up a photo of Bruce at a pumpkin patch, one of those vacant lots that sell pumpkins in October before switching to Christmas trees in November and December. He is sitting on a bale of hay, looking directly into the camera. Although I'm sure he was told to smile, he looks vaguely anxious. You can tell by the way his mouth turns down a little at the corners.

Whenever I look at this picture, I realize how much I will never know about him.

* * *

A few years ago, in response to our mother's questions about what he had done that day, Bruce claimed not to have done anything but watch TV. The person taking care of him, indignant, said that he had taken Bruce to several places: McDonald's, the grocery store, the park. My mother was angry at the caregiver, calling him lazy. Her son would never deceive her, she said. But secretly, I hoped that the man was right, that my brother was normal enough to lie.

* * *

"I wish," Ellie says, a few months after the abortion, "that I hadn't scattered the baby's ashes."

"Why?" I ask. I remember how relieved she had felt to dust the ashes into the Pacific. *Cleansing*, she had said at the time. *Closure.*

"It would be nice to at least have a box. Something to remind me that the baby actually existed. Even if for only a few months."

* * *

Retard. Moron. Idiot. Slow. Dummy. Mongoloid. Half-wit. Backward. Feeble-minded. Weak-minded.

Roget's is careful to precede these words—the few synonyms for *retardation* that it includes—with the italicized word "offensive." For the words *autism* and *autistic*, though, it comes up empty.

* * *

Christmas, 1981. I walk by my brother's bedroom as our father gets him ready for bed. Out of the corner of my eye, I glimpse a confusion of arms, a flash of an elbow raised at an unfamiliar angle. Our father's voice has a tone I usually don't hear, the tone of a passive person suddenly feeling a surge of power. Further down the hall, I allow myself to name what I have seen—my father, hitting my brother.

(Even trying to write about this, I feel disconnected from my body. Suddenly the words stop. So much easier to stop writing, shut the computer down. To shut down. To say: I won't say that. I didn't see that. Better to show mastery. The mastery he'll never have.)

* * *

Whenever I reread *The Sound and the Fury*, I feel it—the burning behind my eyes and pressure in my throat that I recognize as signs of buried tears. But I never give in to them. They won't change anything. Because every time I pick up the book, Benjy will still be bellowing. Caddy will still be there and not-there, failing Benjy forever by disappearing into her own life. I hate Benjy for making me cry, for making me feel anything at all. But I hate Caddy even more. For tending to Benjy when no one else would. For finally leaving him behind. For making me feel that I don't love Bruce enough. For reminding me that I can't leave him behind.

* * *

My father, who believes in the power of reason, is not inclined to describe his dreams. But once, years ago, he told us about a dream he'd had the previous night, in which my brother was playing college football. He was a rookie, but still, when the ball came his way, he snatched it and ran up the field. Bigger players lunged at him, but he dodged and weaved for a few yards until finally being tackled just shy of the 30-yard line. Listening to my father, I felt a sudden surge of jealousy. I may be the normal one, the child of voice recitals and good report cards, but I can never take my place along the line of scrimmage, never burst into the end zone, never have my father slap me on the back after a game. It is only years later that I understand the dream's secret: my father's disappointment. He cannot forgive my brother for the betrayal of autism.

* * *

As a child, I defended Bruce against other kids who called him a retard. "That's not true!" I would say. "He is *not* a retard! You don't understand! He's autistic!" I used the same word, the big one my parents had taught me, when explaining my brother to teachers and neighbors. Sometimes, in that pre-*Rain Man* era, one of them would reply, "Oh! Does he draw?"

* * *

It's a rainy day in October, four months after Ellie's abortion. We're sitting across from each other in a coffeehouse, the kind with worn armchairs and scratched wooden tables. We've gotten together to discuss why we don't seem to get together more often, why we don't talk as much as we used to. Secretly, I know the answer: we thought we were the same, and then we realized we weren't. An unborn baby came between us. And yet I wonder: if my only choice were a child with autism or none at all, what would I do? I don't want even to imagine the question. But it hovers, unanswered, nonetheless.

* * *

"Candace." Mother said. Caddy stooped and lifted me. We staggered. "Candace." Mother said.

"Hush." Caddy said. "You can still see it. Hush."

"Bring him here." Mother said. "He's too big for you to carry. You must stop trying. You'll injure your back. All of our women have prided themselves on their carriage. Do you want to look like a washerwoman."

"He's not too heavy." Caddy said. "I can carry him."

* * *

Next to the photo of Bruce in the pumpkin patch is a Thanksgiving card he made for me. At the top of the card are some tentatively drawn turkey feathers. Below them, he has printed "Happy Thanksgiving Erika." The letters are wobbly, like the leg movements of someone just learning to skate. They've been there for months, but I still notice them every time I walk in and out of the kitchen, the way a mother never stops noticing her child playing in a corner of the room. As if I were a mother, putting my child's first wiggles of writing on the refrigerator in an unthinking gesture of faith.

Visiting Becky

3

Anne Clinard Barnhill

What I remember most is the sound of Mother's voice as it filtered through the wooden floor up to my second-story bedroom, dipping and curving about in the air, much like the road that led to our old house on top of Grab-A-Nickel Hill, the asphalt hugging the mountain in that same haphazard way. I couldn't understand any of the words, but I recognized the tunes, hymns mostly—"In the Garden," "The Old Rugged Cross."

Her singing jarred me, tipped me over to the edge of my bed. I hated how her thin trill imitated the women who performed solos at church. Ever since I'd turned twelve, I'd been mad at the world, especially angry at anyone happy enough to warble with no care for anyone else's ears. I couldn't explain the rage, but most of it was directed at Mother and her constant barrage of music. Maybe it had something to do with my little sister, Becky, being shipped away.

I couldn't tolerate the way Mother's sound lingered in my brain, the echo of her whiny voice following me to school and even out onto the playground. And I especially hated the way she woke me up each day. I'd hear her shift songs on her way up the stairs, going from a hymn to Handel's *Messiah*, a wispy rendition of "Arise, Shine, for Thy Light Is Come." She was pleased with her wit, but after what seemed like a thousand mornings, the joke got old.

Everything was a song with her; at least, that's how it seemed to me. I don't remember exactly when the singing started, maybe the year Becky went away, maybe before. Most of the time, Mother stuck to the familiar hymns. But every once in a while, she'd launch into a Beatles' song—"I Wanna Hold Your Hand" and "She Loves You." She'd increase the volume on the "yeah, yeah, yeah," parts until it was all I could do to keep from telling her to shut the hell up. I'd only begun to notice some of the other kids using cuss words, and I hadn't said any out loud. But in my mind I thought them and got a little thrill each time I found an appropriate occasion for one.

It seemed forever since she actually spoke to me, except to remind me of my homework or to tell me to do the dishes. I could keep track of her easily by listening for her song and gauge the exact moment before she'd be at my door to check on my progress with math. The system worked well. It allowed me plenty of time to put away my library book and take out pencil and paper, then plaster a studious look on my face before she peered in at me.

When I came downstairs for a snack, I could see her bending over the table in the living room with a can of furniture polish in one hand, my old underwear in the other, singing, "This is my story / this is my song / Praising my Savior / all the day long." Over and over she'd sing, a crazy litany, her weak soprano scraping along, marking each hour of the day.

At first it didn't bother me so much. I figured this love affair with notes and measures would pass like some flu bug. But the singing didn't go away. Rather, it grew, and by most evenings, my mother's voice sounded hoarse and ragged. I spent as much time away from home as I could.

Mostly, I explored the woods behind our house. One spring, I discovered all kinds of new growth: the tiny bluets, each blossom smaller than my fingernail, yet perfect, the blue darkening at the edges, a yellow star at the center; and the laurel, heavy white-and-purple buds hanging on dark, waxy leaves, the bushes creating secret places, shadowy habitats for rabbits and ground squirrels. I watched as the mountains slowly turned from brown to new green under the clear April sky.

And I was happy to skip along trails made by the neighborhood kids and watch the sun streak through the trees, splotches of light and dark that fit together tight as puzzle pieces. I liked puzzles. They made sense to me. Sometimes they were the only thing that did, and I felt better after putting together a jigsaw alone in my room, like I'd somehow improved the world by taking the jagged parts and linking them to create a beautiful picture.

But Mother's singing disturbed the peace I created for myself, irritating me the way a mosquito bite will itch its way under your skin and go all red and puffy. I still recall how my muscles would tense up each time I heard her. Even now, when I hear a certain melody, I think back about what it was like then, growing up with my mother's voice lifted in song, my little sister torn away from us as surely as if Death itself had grabbed her.

Becky was only six years old when she went to live in a group home a state away. She was cute with long blond curls and clear blue eyes. I'd waited such a long time for a sister, six whole years; by the time I got Becky, I was old enough to take care of her the same way I'd rocked and patted my doll babies. She was almost like a doll herself, tiny and delicate, much smaller than I was when I was little. In my baby pictures, I was a kid with sprigs of brown, straight hair poking out in odd directions. I had shiny round cheeks that the kids at school used to call "chipmunk cheeks." It was true; they looked stuffed full of something. I hated the way they bulged out, but at least I made mostly A's on my tests. It was my one consolation. I was smart. But I'd rather have had a delicate face and a small, upturned nose like Becky's.

Of course, she paid a price for her good looks, and my brains cost me, too. We both gained something, lost something. I didn't know who was keeping tabs, but balancing things out was important to somebody.

At first, I wasn't sure just how far from normal my sister was. I mean, my friends had siblings who did some pretty bizarre things, like the time Mike Robin's brother jumped from the roof of the house onto the shed and broke his leg. He was pretending to be what he called the Amazing Frog Boy. Of course, no one had ever heard of Frog Boy, and we all thought the kid was a little strange. But Becky was worse than that. Each day I noticed something new that stamped Becky as odd.

She didn't eat the way the other kids her age ate. She wouldn't touch candy or cookies, things most children love. The only thing she really liked was "peachers" and "begetables and beeth." Baby food. At four, she was still eating it straight from the jar. And she talked to herself all the time, asking and answering her own questions in a way that sounded like music. I knew she wasn't like the other kids long before my parents took me into the doctor's office to have him explain it. I knew by the way the other kids left her out and she didn't even mind. She was in her own little world where no one else could enter. Except me. Sometimes I could join her, though not often, but I learned early on to take what I could get.

As if all those clues weren't enough, Becky gave me another to make sure I knew she was something special. It happened one Saturday afternoon when all the kids were playing in the sunshine on our dead-end street. Whenever Mother sent us outside, my job was to keep an eye on Becky. She stayed in the yard most of the time, flipping a ball up in the air and talking in a low voice to herself. I anchored myself close by. But sometimes I'd forget about Becky. I was busy playing freeze tag or Cowboys and Indians.

Every kid in the neighborhood knew not to go into Old Man Green's perfectly manicured yard. I'd told Becky about Old Man Green many times, and she usually listened to me and stayed away. This day she forgot.

Green didn't have any children, a rare thing in our neighborhood. And he hated kids. He'd chase any living creature out of his yard with a baseball bat that he kept handy on his front porch. If somebody accidentally threw a ball into his shrubs, it stayed there until it rotted. And the best way to get even with an enemy was to toss his favorite toy into the flower garden. The victim could kiss it good-bye forever.

Imagine how I felt when I was playing four square in the road with a bunch of my friends when suddenly I saw Becky charging into the forbidden zone with the zeal of a bull elephant. I ran from my hard-earned spot in the server's square to grab her before she went too far.

But I was clumsy and slow: before I knew it, she'd plodded right into Old Man Green's tulips, trampling the heavy buds as she went. By the time I reached her, Old Man Green had his bat in hand, and his red face huffed swear words at us both.

"If she's too goddam dumb to stay out of my yard, then you'd better keep her out. You hear?" His spittle fell on my upturned face. No grown-up had cussed at me before.

"Let's get out of here, Becky. He's mean," I said in the strongest voice I could muster. I didn't care if he chased me with his bat. He'd called Becky dumb. I'd never let anyone call her that. And he acted like there was something wrong with me, too. He lumped us together, and I didn't like it. I knew I wasn't like her, but I wondered if something in me might get crazy, some hidden thing that might pop out as suddenly as chicken pox. When he raised his bat to threaten us, anger propelled me out of his yard faster than I thought I could go. And I dragged Becky behind me by her skinny arm.

"Don't ever go in there again. He's a bad man. *A bad man.* Understand?" I shook her shoulders just a little for emphasis. She wouldn't look at me, but that wasn't unusual. I could tell she'd already gone somewhere else, her eyes fixed far away. She gritted her teeth, a habit she'd had since the first tiny row of seed pearls appeared on her gums. "Stop gritting." Already she'd worn them down so that they were angled funny. I was trying to break her of it.

Each afternoon when I came home from school, I'd find Mother and Becky working at the kitchen table. Mother was trying to teach Becky how to count to ten, her ABC's, and her colors. I'd throw my books on the counter, grab a glass of cold milk, eat a couple of cookies, and do my homework right then to get it out of the way. Sometimes I thought I'd go nuts if I heard the alphabet song one more time, but Becky was getting it, and she'd learned to sing it all the way through. Now Mother was helping her learn what the letters looked like. Becky tried hard, and sometimes I could almost forget the strange stuff she did. I'd look at her little cute face, the blond curls, the sweet smile, and I'd almost have myself believing she'd be all right.

Becky might have looked like a little angel, but she didn't always act like one. Sometimes living with her wasn't easy. One day after school I raced home to catch the popular western *Bonanza* on television. It was the episode where Hoss finds leprechauns, and I couldn't wait. I took the stairs two at a time so I could change into my play clothes and plop in front of the old black-and-white TV set in my mother's bedroom. When I opened the door to my room, I couldn't believe what I saw. Scattered over my floor were doll parts—arms, legs, heads, torsos—and standing in the middle of the mess was Becky, sort of jumping in place. She held the head of my bride doll by its golden hair and was flipping her fingers against the plastic face. Bridey's eyes blinked open, then snapped shut with each new attack.

"*Mom*! I'm going to *kill* Becky!" My voice tore from my throat, and I stepped quickly over the mutilated toys to save my Bridey, or what was left of her. I screamed again at Becky, but she didn't do anything. All she did was stand there and look at me like there was nothing strange in that room, nothing malicious in her act of destruction.

"What's the matter?" Mother stood at the doorway, her hands covered in flour. Then she took a look around. "Oh, my God." Mother's face turned white; for a minute, she didn't say a word. Her eyes reminded me of caged birds, wild and looking for a way out. Then she put her arms around me and whispered.

"She didn't mean to... She doesn't know any better." She stooped over to retrieve Bridey's legs, which were protruding from her wedding dress. "I'll get your daddy to fix this." Mother patted my back for a long time. Finally, she turned to me, her hand still on my shoulder and said, "Don't be mad at her." She left the two of us there, and I heard her humming softly as she went back to the kitchen. "Stay with Becky. Don't leave her by herself," she called to me from downstairs.

I stared at Becky, the fury still in me. She looked down at her hands and started giggling. It was a zany kind of laugh, full of the devil, as my grandmother would have said. And then she started talking to herself in that strange melodic way she had. She never referred to herself in the first person but kept a safe third-person distance.

"Is her sister mad at her? Does her sister want to kill her? Her sister's angry. Why is her sister angry?" Over and over under her breath until I felt my heart soften, go to a sort of mush.

"It's okay, Becky. I'm not mad. I'm not." I pulled her to me, and she stood stiff while I hugged her.

Soon after the doll incident, my parents sent Becky away. They told me there were special doctors in Pittsburgh who knew just what to do with kids like Becky. They told me the doctors could help Becky become more normal. I wanted that more than anything, so I tried not to cry that first time when my parents and Becky headed for Pennsylvania. I couldn't go along because school was still in session. I didn't mind missing the trip because I didn't want to tell Becky good-bye. Besides, I really liked Mrs. Talley, my babysitter.

The following Tuesday, I didn't hurry home after school, even though I knew Mother would be back. Instead, I followed the path through the woods, then struck my own trail and discovered a meadow at the top of the hill. I stood at the edge and lost myself in the sweet sunshine. I stood for a long time, the light washing over me. I thought about Becky and why she was the way she was. I wondered why God did stuff to little kids. I tried to lay blame, but there wasn't any place to put it.

Exhausted, I hiked home, my clothes hot and growing sticky with sweat. Finally, I headed for my own yard, my own room. I heard Mother as I reached the mailbox at the end of the driveway.

"Oh, Soul, are you weary and troubled? / No light in the darkness you see / Turn your eyes upon Jesus." Her voice was rough, gravelly, and it sounded as if she'd been singing forever. She was cooking pot roast, peeling potatoes and cutting onions. I watched from the kitchen door as she wiped her wet cheek with the back of her arm, her knife in one hand, the onion in the other.

That night at supper, I was afraid to mention Becky, terrified of what might happen if her name was spoken. My parents acted cheerful, but I noticed they didn't eat much, and they, too, said nothing of their trip to Pittsburgh.

I wanted Becky to get well, to be like all the other little kids. I kept that picture of her in my mind, of us growing up together, me giving her advice about boys, discussing our weird parents, laughing and giggling in our room after we'd been told to settle down and go to sleep. Part of me knew it was impossible, but another part believed in miracles.

I took to praying. I don't mean just occasional prayer spoken off the top of my head. I mean "deliberate petition." I learned about tenacity in Sunday school when the teacher told us about the widow who kept bugging a certain judge for justice until he finally gave in, just so she'd shut up. That's the kind of praying I did for Becky. I wanted justice for her, and there wasn't anything fair about her being sent away and her being "different."

I begged God until my throat hurt and my eyes made wet spots on my pillow. My ears clogged and my hair was damp from the tears, and still I prayed. I imagined my prayers rising up to heaven, a silver stream of words washing over the ears of all the angels, trickling into the very ear of God himself. My prayers would sound like the sweetest music, and his ear would lap them up.

I didn't let up because Becky's life depended on it. I had to plead hard, and most nights I prayed myself to sleep.

I remembered the story about the woman who touched the hem of Jesus's garment. She didn't really bother the Lord. Instead, she almost stole her healing away from him. That's what I wanted Becky to do: steal up to Jesus and swipe at his robe. If she could just touch it, she'd be healed.

So far, though I was faithful in beseeching the Lord on her behalf, nothing had changed. Becky still flipped her doll heads; she still ground her teeth and chattered to herself in that sing-song way. But maybe the special school would be the answer, just as Dad said. Maybe she could reach out and grab Jesus's garment in Pittsburgh.

Later that summer, Dad, Mother and I packed up the camper to visit Becky. I didn't know what to expect. We were going for Becky's birthday. She was turning six, and she'd been at the group home for almost four months.

We'd only talked about Becky once since she'd been gone. My dad explained that, no matter how hard it was to leave Becky, no matter how much we missed her, we had to give the group home a try. He said when you really love someone, you do what's best for that person, not what feels best for yourself.

I kept wondering what it would be like to leave home, to be without your family. I couldn't imagine. The thought of going away scared me, and I couldn't stand the idea of being away from my parents. I thought I'd even miss Mother's singing. Well, maybe. I didn't dare try to put myself in Becky's shoes.

Though I wouldn't let myself think about how she must feel, sometimes quick-crazy images flashed through my mind. Becky sitting alone in her room. Or crying into her pillow. Or being punished without me there to comfort her. I worried about her gritting her teeth more than ever.

* * *

On that first trip, Mother woke me early. As usual, she sang, but on this special day, she veered from her routine and wandered into new territory—Negro spirituals.

"Are you ready for the kingdom? Oh yeah." She stuck her round face into my room, her mouth pretty with bright lipstick. She snapped her fingers in rhythm to the gospel song.

"I'm getting up. Give me time." My anger seeped out everywhere, and my voice clenched up its fist. That year, I had a hard time controlling it. "Do you have to sing?" I mumbled this last part, afraid I'd hurt her feelings by mentioning the weird habit. Usually, I didn't mind causing Mother pain, but I didn't want to spoil the weekend. I wanted everything to be perfect for Becky.

I hurried once Mother had left me to myself and slipped on the outfit I'd chosen. The red skirt was new, and I wore a matching striped blouse. At the store, Mother had insisted that the skirt skim the tops of my knees, which was way longer than the other girls wore theirs. But though the skirt was longer than I liked, I wore it anyway because red was Becky's favorite color. And besides, Becky didn't care whether my skirt was the fashionable length or not. All she cared about was seeing me, seeing the whole family.

I was looking forward to spending the night in our pop-up camper. Becky would take the top bunk, and I'd sleep below her. Each night I'd tell her stories. My words would weave us together, and we'd laugh at the cockeyed tales. Becky liked scary ones and funny ones, so with each story I tried to outdo myself. I thought all week about what I'd say. For sure, the spooky "Who's Got My Talie Toe" and maybe one about dental hygiene. Becky considered teeth funny and loved to hear about visits to the dentist.

When we were together, Becky would call me "Jet," her pet name for me. She explained that she thought my face was shaped like a jet airplane, but I didn't see it. Jets were angular and sleek, and my face didn't fit such a description. But I was happy she saw me that way, and I looked forward to hearing her sing her original composition, "Jet-Shaped Face." She made it up all by herself with what she called her "musical ears."

While we packed the car, my parents acted like we were going to an amusement park or some such thing. Of course, we *were* planning to go to Kennywood Park where there was a huge rollercoaster. Becky loved those things, though you'd have thought she'd have been afraid of them. She used to smile each time the train would climb up to the sky, then hurl us toward the earth. She'd scream and scream, and the minute we hopped off, she wanted to get on again. I couldn't wait to try the one at Kennywood.

Dad told me there was a zoo also. When we went to the dinky French Creek Animal Farm in West Virginia, Becky liked the petting zoo in particular, where she could actually touch the animals. The last time we went, she followed a billy goat around forever, pulling its tail down to cover its butt. She liked a sense of order, everything in its place. I knew the Pittsburgh zoo would be a lot better, and I wondered what Becky would do when she saw exotic animals like elephants and lions.

But though we were planning to do fun things, I knew the activities were mostly for Becky. And I didn't understand why my folks forced such a festive mood during the journey. For me, the trip meant a knot in my stomach and tears threatening at the back of my throat. And the dread of saying good-bye to Becky once more.

She was waiting at the door when we got there, her hair cut short and blunt, the curls gone. Her face was red and roughened by the sun, her shirttail out on one side and the plaid skirt she wore hiked up in the back. She'd never liked skirts, but I guess she, too, wanted to dress up. Or maybe they made her.

A fat woman dressed in a white uniform stood guard beside her, one large black hand on Becky's small shoulder. Becky started toward us the minute she saw us walking in from the parking lot, but I saw that hand restrain her. When we reached the door, the woman could no longer hold her, and she rushed to us, threw her arms around Mother. Mother held her, the longest hug I'd ever seen her give. Then Becky embraced Dad, and, finally, me.

The nurse led us to Becky's room, one she shared with another girl. Her weekend bag was packed. Gunbaby, her favorite doll, poked out from the top of the zipper. Gunbaby was the only doll that hadn't had his head ripped off. He was all of a piece and looked something like Daniel Boone with breeches and a rifle molded along with his regular body parts. No way could Becky pull that head off.

Other kids gathered at Becky's doorway. They watched, their eyes wild and strange, as we picked up the suitcase and started to leave.

"Where going? Where?" said one little boy with bright orange hair. I watched, stared, even though I knew it wasn't polite, as his head jerked to one side over and over. The big girl behind him sucked her thumb and drool oozed down her chin.

"Home? Go home?" Yet another face intruded, a black girl about thirteen. My age. Her hair was matted into short pigtails and she wore a striped shirt with plaid slacks. I cringed at the combination.

Suddenly, I wanted out of there. The air was too hot, too thick with people. Becky seemed to disappear, blend into this strange collection. It was hard to tell her from the others. I didn't want her to be a part of this gang of weirdos. I wanted her to be with us, Mother, Dad, and me. I pushed through the little cluster, and Becky followed me.

She ignored them all. She didn't even notice when the boy with the nodding head grabbed my hand. She hurried for the front door, full speed ahead. My hand was gooey from where the redhead held onto me, gripping me tight until the nurse made him let go. I brushed my sticky fingers against the new skirt and ran with Becky to the car.

That night for supper we ate at McDonald's. Mother worried about what Becky might find to eat there, and we were all surprised when she said she wanted fries and a milkshake.

"I didn't know you liked french fries, honey. That's great. I'm glad you're trying new things." Mother smiled, and Dad tussled Becky's hair with his big palm. She and I dipped our fries in ketchup and slurped our chocolate shakes. I watched as hope bloomed across Mother's features while Becky gobbled up real food. I, too, thought maybe my prayers were being answered.

"What do you do at the group home, Becky?" I wanted to know if she was getting better or if it was just my imagination.

"Her sister wants to know what she does. Her sister asked her a question. Ballet? Does she take ballet?" Becky answered me as usual, more with a question than an answer, but I knew what she meant.

"That's great. Ballet, huh. Can you show me a dance?" I didn't mean for her to demonstrate in the restaurant. That she might hadn't even occurred to me. But before we could stop her, she was pirouetting around the place, and every eye was on her. She didn't care. On and on she spun, all over the restaurant, bumping into people, spilling drinks, until Dad caught her by the elbow and pulled her back to our table.

Mother shushed her, and Becky began to cry. The fries I'd eaten sank like cement in my stomach.

* * *

The weekend passed quickly; soon the time came to say our good-byes. I would learn that the time always came.

Dad swung into the lot in front of Becky's building and parked in the visitor slot. Seeing that word, "Visitor," printed in white on the curb made me feel funny, like we weren't a real family. My lunch sloshed around in my stomach. Becky begged for another story as Dad turned off the engine.

"We don't have time, honey. Gotta get on the road. Gotta get home before dark." His thin, brown hair fell across his face when he turned to talk to us in the back seat. He pushed it away with his hand, and I noticed his skin was grayish, the color of dustballs under my bed. Mother was quiet.

"Just one more. Please. I can make it short." I pleaded, my voice whiny.

"No. Not this time." He answered in his no-nonsense voice, and I realized I'd lost. I grabbed Becky's hand as she pulled on the door handle. We scooted out together.

We walked behind Mother and Dad. Both of us dawdled, dragging our feet, stopping to smell the flowers that lined the sidewalk. I didn't want to leave her, not here, not with all those loonies. She didn't belong. Why didn't anyone see that but me? She was smarter than those other kids and so much prettier. She didn't drool.

My stomach tightened.

Becky led us to her room where Mother put her clean, folded clothes away in the dresser drawer. While she worked, she and Becky sang silly songs. This time Mother's singing didn't bother me. I even joined in and did the motions with Becky for "I'm a Little Teapot." Becky showed us some of her drawings, told us about her ballet lessons and demonstrated the positions. Mother finally finished with the clothes, snapped the lid of the empty suitcase shut and shoved it under Becky's bed. Mother's cheeks looked sunken; even her red lipstick didn't do much to brighten her face. She spoke in a whisper.

"That about does it," she said soft as a lullaby.

Dad wrapped Becky in his arms, made a shell of himself around her. "Give me a big hug." Becky held on long and tight. She'd never been one for hugs and kisses, but she'd learned to allow them, even the really extended touches. Now she made a show of her kisses, stretching her arms open and smacking her lips with a loud, wet noise.

After Dad was finished, Mother cupped Becky's small cheeks in her hands. They gazed at each other.

"When can Becky come home, Mommy? Becky wants to come home." Becky's eyes teared up, and Mother stood speechless. Dad reached to take Becky into his lap. He didn't look at Mother, who seemed unable to move.

"They're trying to help you, Becky. Help you learn. You work hard and you'll be home soon. I promise." His voice broke just a little. Mother turned her back to us.

Finally, it was my turn to say good-bye. I held Becky, my eyes squeezed together hard.

"Bye, Jet," she yelled in my ear. I felt Dad's hand on my shoulder, the signal to let her go.

* * *

By the time I'd curled myself into a ball in the back seat of the car, my head pounded. Dad backed out of the parking space, and I unrolled myself to wave to Becky one last time. She stood inside the storm door of the building, the same fat nurse beside her, that hand again on her shoulder. Dad began to drive away very slowly.

Suddenly, Becky broke loose from the nurse, opened the door, and ran after the car. She was all arms and legs flailing in the air. I stared, unable to believe she was following us, unable to tear my eyes from her small body framed by the rear window.

"Dad! Stop the car! She's running after us. Stop!" I heard him suck in his breath; then he looked into the rearview mirror. His throat made a loud sound as he swallowed. Mother hunched her shoulders just a little. She stared ahead.

Dad didn't respond. He kept driving the same slow pace as when he started. I watched as the nurse lumbered after Becky, caught her, and bound her in those large, black arms. We drove on.

No one spoke. We didn't utter a word for the whole trip home. We were wrapped in silence, eggshell-thin. A sound would have broken us.

On the Way to the Sky

Katie Harrington Stricklin

4

I do not remember the first time I heard the word *autism*. Nor do I recall a time in my life that I ever really understood what the word meant. Perhaps it was easier for me growing up that way; perhaps it is still easier for me that way now. Whatever the case may be, my experience with autism stems not from desire or choice but rather from necessity. My only brother Doug has autism.

* * *

Most of my early childhood I recall only through stories told to me by my parents. We are able to laugh at many of those stories now, but at the time I know they brought mostly tears. I understand that I played an instrumental role in getting Doug to talk at an early age. One day I asked him a question, and I imagine that, like most of the time, there was no reply. I guess I really wanted an answer that day because I proceeded to hit him until he gave me a response. Now, I do not recall this exact incident, but I do not recall ever again needing to resort to violence to get

Doug to talk either. The next time I asked him a question I guess he knew I meant business.

When I sit down to reminisce about other facets of my childhood with Doug, the things I seem to recall most often are the things that made me sad, things I never could have possibly understood at the time. I recall, for example, watching Doug pace back and forth wearing a path in the grass on the side of our Missouri house. I once thought this was just his special place and time to get away from the trials of childhood. Then I realized that he would spend hours on end pacing, usually tapping a weed in his left hand. He rarely said a word to anyone; he rarely took his eyes off the ground. I wondered what he thought about. Did he think about us, his family? Did he think about the day that was almost over? Or did he think about nothing at all? I never asked him, probably because watching him made me feel lonely and I was afraid his answer would be the latter of the three possibilities.

I remember a time riding home on the school bus. Kids would tease and poke fun at Doug the entire way home. Was I to stand up for him, or could he defend himself? One day my question was answered when he had taken all he could handle and hit a kid over the head with his *Dukes of Hazzard* lunch box. Now, I'm not sure which hurt more, the kid's head or his ego, but he could not have been more embarrassed than I was. Did I have the right to feel this way when deep down my heart had been torn a little further apart with each joke about Doug? Should I have been standing beside him cheering because he, for once, had the last word? All my questions that will be forever unanswered I raise only now, at the age of thirty-five.

There are endless stories I could tell that raise these unanswered questions about my relationship with my brother, but that is not my sole purpose in writing this essay. The stories, although demonstrating my experience with autism, are simply an account of my life's journey on the way to the sky. It is my hope this essay will help me finally to find resolution in my own mind, to know that perhaps I made as big an impact in Doug's life as he has made in mine.

Autism is a topic that I never discussed with anyone outside my family—never. I attribute this to the fact that my parents at no time made an issue of Doug's being any different from me or from any other kid on the block. Doug and I were treated equally by our parents in all respects. I do remember there were times when it seemed Doug would monopolize their attention. My turn would always come around, though. My dad and I would go on special "dates," which would usually end up at my favorite Chinese restaurant. I would also spend "quality time" with my mom, which customarily entailed shopping in the small downtown square of Kirksville, Missouri.

The individual attention I received from my parents was special to me. They were always just as involved in my activities as they were in Doug's. What stands out in my mind now, however, was the time that we spent together as a family, which in the early years often centered around something Doug was doing. I remember a time when Doug had to do nightly exercises called Cross-Crawls to pattern the left and right hemispheres of the brain. At the time, I had no idea of their purpose, but each night I would join in. We would make it a family event right before we said our prayers. I never once felt left out.

As the seasons changed, the years passed from one to the next; Doug and I grew older. I know that living in Kirksville, Missouri, was hard for Doug through his junior high years. Getting picked on by the popular crowd was part of Doug's daily routine. He had matured, though, and many days he was able just to ignore the ridicule. It seemed, however, that he still spent his share of time in in-house suspension for the days he could not handle the frustration. He was not involved in many activities, nor did he have many friends. Since he was two years younger, my friends and I did not always want Doug following us around, so he was included only when we hung out at my house. Doug did feel left out.

I recall the two years we spent together at Kirksville Junior High School as being a very difficult time for me as well. None of my friends ever asked about Doug or why he did what he did, but I know they always wondered. I could have explained Doug's behavior with just one word, *autism*, but I never did. I had this gut feeling that if the word were out in the open, it would have been used to hurt Doug even more. I did not want that. Instead, I kept it all to myself. I just let my friends wonder why Doug was different.

In the summer before my freshman year of high school, my family moved to Las Vegas, Nevada. Doug, surprisingly, had the most resistance to the move. It turned out to be the best thing that could have ever happened to him and to our family. In Las Vegas, specifically at Chaparral High School, there were no history, no past, no remembering Doug as the one who hit some kid with his lunch box. It was a fresh start.

I am possibly the most thankful for our move to Las Vegas of any of my family. Knowing no one besides my family that first summer, Doug and I grew closer. We both got involved in our church youth group and made new friends—together. When school started, we were both in band and made new friends— together. Throughout high school, Doug was included in many things that my friends and I did as a group. If I did not ask him to join in, someone else usually would. Despite Doug's peculiar social behavior, he was accepted and he was liked. Once again, I am sure our friends wondered why Doug did what he did, but no one ever asked, so I never told.

I would like to think I came to a better understanding about Doug after our move to Las Vegas, but perhaps Doug came to a better understanding about life. All I know is that I have very few sad memories of Doug since we left Missouri. There were still hard times in high school, though. There were dances, activities, dates, and games that Doug never attended. He showed interest in only a few girls and was rejected by each. I would like to say, "if only they understand." That is not fair of me, though. It has taken me thirty-five years to understand. I can only have faith that one day someone will understand.

Although I have no professional or technical training with respect to autism, I know there is no cure. There is, however, patience, persistence, and love. Doug was lucky to be born to parents who demonstrate all three each and every day. Having experienced firsthand the progress Doug has made throughout his life has only reinforced my belief in the power of prayers, goals, dreams, and early intervention, which in the early 1970s was not easy to come by. In 1990, Doug graduated from Chaparral High School with a class rank of 72 out of 422. Today, Doug is employed full time at a premier resort on the Las Vegas Strip in the steward department. Although he still lives with our parents, he drives, pays taxes, and enjoys life.

After I graduated from the University of Nevada, Las Vegas, I moved away to pursue career goals of my own. Doug never said this in so many words, but I know he was sad. He has been to visit me several times in Southern California and I hope that he now has a better understanding of why I did what I did. It is funny how the questions never really go away; the tables merely turn.

To this day, I still cannot tell you whether autism is classified as an illness, disease, or syndrome. It does not really matter to me, though, nor do all the textbook definitions, medical interpretations, or scientific hypotheses still waiting to be proven. What matters to me is my brother Doug, who has autism. I am glad Doug is my brother. He has taught me to laugh and to cry at all life has to offer—to value each day on the way to the sky.

Victim of Silence 5

Ann E. Damiano

I absolutely hated when my mother picked me up from elementary school. Usually I rode to and from St. Anthony's School in a lurching, grinding, yellow school bus, the owner's name, "Peter Brega," painted in black letters on its side. If I stayed after school for some activity, though, my mother had to pick me up. She drove an old Dodge, a clunky, early-1950s mint-green car with rounded edges she had inherited from her father when he died. That car was nothing like the sleek, angular Chevy Impalas, Ford Country Station Wagons, or Buick Skylarks other kids' parents drove. My mother affectionately referred to her car as "Old Betsy."

The minute I spotted Old Betsy coming into the school's parking lot, I bolted out the door, hoping my classmates, especially the really cool kids, wouldn't notice the car I was getting into. But it wasn't just the car. Sitting in the front passenger seat, rocking to some mysterious tune in his head, was my older brother Danny— my older, profoundly autistic brother. I didn't want anyone to see him. My reason was very simple: Danny made me different from everyone else. I wanted to fit in with my peers, and the way to fit in was to be just like them, maybe even a little bit better.

In eighth grade, I was cast as Aunt Martha in my school's production of *Arsenic and Old Lace*. Practices were scheduled after school about three times a week, beginning in late winter and extending into early spring, when the days were golden brown, purple crocuses covered the lawn outside the rectory, skunk cabbage poked through the marshy land next to the convent, and we all wanted to do something else besides recite memorized lines on a dusty stage in a stuffy auditorium.

One afternoon, Sister Maureen James, the play's director and my eighth-grade English teacher, asked me to stay after practice to work on blocking a scene. When she finally dismissed me, ten minutes later than usual, I grabbed my books and sweater from backstage and ran to the auditorium doors. A crowd of kids had gathered there, some snickering, others squealing with unrestrained laughter. Not everyone. Billy McGuire, standing aloof from the crowd, looked at me sympathetically. So did Maureen Conlon. Tommy Donahue, though, captured everyone's attention, both the cool kids and the not-so-cool kids. He entertained them all, rocking back and forth, waving his hand in front of his face, saying in a garbled voice, "Look at me! I'm a retard."

"Ann," one girl hiccupped. "Your mother's here for you!"

She exploded with suppressed hilarity, peppering my face with her saliva. Her laughter deteriorated into snorts and grunts. She sounded like a pig. Her eyes, squinted into slits, made her look like one, too.

"Who's the guy in the front seat, the one next to your mother?" John Koptula asked.

"Shouldn't he be in the loony bin?"

"Yeah, what about Letchworth?"

Their laughter crested into a raucous, harmonious chorus of derision.

My entire body, especially my face, felt scorched. My intestines tied themselves into a tight knot, and it felt as if a vise were strangling my parched throat. In my peripheral vision, I watched Tommy Donahue poke his tongue out of the corner of his mouth and stumble around stupidly. Sounds became muffled. I walked toward the auditorium doors, moving in what was like a slow-motion swim through murky water. My classmates morphed into indistinct, bluish shadowy forms.

With limbs almost too heavy to lift, I climbed into the back seat of Old Betsy.

It didn't matter that the girl who first talked to me had a terrible case of acne, angry purplish-red cysts erupting on her cheeks. It didn't matter that the guy who said Danny belonged in a loony bin was born with a cleft lip that some surgeon did a lousy job repairing. It didn't matter that Tommy Donahue was placed in the lowest reading group for all eight years in Saint Anthony's School. Neither did it matter that I had the lead role in the play or the second highest average in my class or that I had won first prize in the school's science competition a month ago for my project on bacterial production. All that mattered was I had to climb into a 1954 mint-green Dodge with a retard rocking in the front seat.

"Hi," said my mother, starting the ignition. The smoke from her cigarette stung my eyes. "Well, you got out late today, eh?"

I huddled in the back seat and said nothing.

She pulled out of the parking lot.

"How was school today?" she asked.

She had the car radio on, and a swing band was playing. Tommy Dorsey, maybe. Some band from the olden days when my parents were young.

"Can't you put on WABC?" I asked. WABC was the rock 'n' roll station broadcast from New York City.

"No," my mother answered. "I can't stand that loud rock 'n' roll you listen to. It's obnoxious!"

"This music is so dumb!"

"Boy, oh boy—you're in some mood."

"Why don't you just leave me alone?" I shouted.

I wanted to cry, but I willed away the tears. I inhaled my sadness until it became a boiling rage inside of me.

I kicked the back of Danny's seat as hard as I could.

"My God! Can't you stop rocking? Just cut it out, you retard!"

I had never called him that before. I heard other kids, usually really cool kids, use the word "retard." "He's such a retard," they'd say about someone who did his homework or scored a 100 percent on a science test. Or they'd say, "This is so retarded!" about something Sister Maureen James wanted us to do. I hated when they used that word. I blushed whenever I heard it, sometimes even felt a little dizzy and sick to my stomach.

Angrily, my mother rolled down Old Betsy's window and threw out her cigarette butt. She switched off the radio.

"You're being very ugly, Ann."

"Shut up," I bellowed. "What'd you have to bring him anyway? Couldn't you leave him home?"

I knew very well that Danny could not be left home alone. I scrunched further down in my seat and kicked the back of Danny's seat a second time. I wished I had the strength to kick harder. I would send him crashing through the windshield.

Danny began to moan deep in his throat. He sounded like a cow lowing.

I stared out the car window at all the recently constructed raised ranches neatly arranged on half-acre parcels in well-organized developments, freshly-painted homes untouched by the grit and grime left over from the recently-departed winter. Someday, I thought, I'm going to live in one of these new houses. It'll be a beautiful home. The living room will be wallpapered with big, bright purple-and-yellow flowers. There will be purple bean-bag chairs in the living room and two sinks in the bathroom.

Danny rocked with maniacal fury. The upholstered seat's springs squeaked every time he leaned forward and each time he crashed back. My legs felt weak and rubbery, as if I had just finished a long swim.

My mother lit another cigarette. Hazy, blue-gray smoke enveloped us in a silence punctuated only by the squeaking springs in the front passenger seat. Old Betsy brought us home.

* * *

About two weeks later, spring burst open with all its colorful glory. Pink and white hyacinth blossomed around the Blessed Mother statue in front of Saint Anthony's School. I inhaled the strong, cloying aroma as I entered the building one Friday morning with my classmates—all sixty of us in gray-and-red plaid uniforms, marching in two straight lines.

The school day started with a homeroom period scheduled from 8:45 a.m. until 9:00 a.m. Sister Lucy Joseph, our homeroom and religion teacher, took attendance, and the principal, Sister John Theresa, made announcements and issued reprimands over the public-address system. Afterward, we said a couple of obligatory prayers, and, by 9:00 a.m., we were primed for religion class.

Every day for eight years, the first half hour of instruction was dedicated to religion. But what and how we were taught changed over the years. In the early grades, we learned a little bit of Church Latin, like *Et cum spiritu tuo* and *Corpus Christi*, and the nuns taught us about hell, purgatory, and limbo. We learned that Baptism washed our souls white and pure, but every time we sinned, a black spot stained them. These black spots could be erased only if we went to Confession. If we didn't confess these transgressions, our souls would become completely black, and black souls were not allowed into heaven. By fourth grade, we memorized the complete *Baltimore Catechism,* learned all the important prayers and major hymns, and paraded out to the playground every May to be part of a living rosary, each child representing a bead.

In eighth grade, there was some talk about sin and the Blessed Trinity, but Sister Lucy Joseph said it was more important for us to develop a sense of social justice. I wasn't sure what she meant by "social justice," but she said we had to have it if we were going to call ourselves true followers of Jesus Christ.

Some days Sister talked about the war in Vietnam, telling us to pray for peace. Then she'd play songs for us, like Pete Seeger's "Where Have All the Flowers Gone?" or Bob Dylan's "The Times They Are A-Changin'." She gave us the words to these songs so we could sing along. I especially liked Bob Dylan's assurance that sons and daughters were beyond their parents' control. If that was social justice, I was all for it.

Sister lectured a lot about how we had to love our brothers, especially brothers of different races. The civil rights movement was in high and sometimes violent gear, following the assassination of the Reverend Dr. Martin Luther King almost two years earlier. Sister Lucy Joseph waged on and on about how black people were just like us, how we were all equal in the eyes of God, how God loved us all, and how we were commanded by Jesus to love each other. All this made logical sense to me, though it remained a bit of an abstraction since the only black people I saw close up in real life—not television life—were the men who collected our garbage every Thursday morning. The musical accompaniment to the "love your brother" lectures was Jackie DeShannon's song "What the World Needs Now Is Love."

Sister also taught us a song that poetically described God's skin color as being black, brown, yellow, red, and white. It was a corny song, but considering I had always been shown pictures of God as an elderly white man with thick, flowing white hair and a soft white beard, the lyrics made me think.

When Sister was in the mood to talk about Jesus, she played the soundtrack to the rock opera *Jesus Christ, Superstar* and required us to sing along.

On this particular Friday, Sister was in her "love-your-brother" mode. She opened religion class by playing the record "Reach Out of the Darkness" by Friends and Lovers.

"Now, children," Sister Lucy Joseph asked when the record finished. "What do the words to this song mean? How do they communicate Jesus's message of love and forgiveness?"

I thought the answer to that question was pretty obvious, so I decided not to raise my hand. I figured I'd let the dumber kids have a chance to answer a question. That seemed the most Christian approach.

Theresa Vitiello shot her hand into the air.

"Well," she began, after Sister acknowledged her, "the song talks about people coming together. And that's what Jesus wants us to do."

"Very good, Theresa!" Sister Lucy Joseph beamed. "Anyone else?"

Since Sister Lucy Joseph had us all pretty well trained in the buzz words of social justice, kids raised their hands and babbled on about loving each other, being a friend to all who are in need, not judging anyone before you get to know him, making an extra effort to be nice to people. Sister was thrilled with these replies.

"Yes, children," she endorsed us with a smile. "But still, we don't always do a good job loving others and helping those in need, do we? We don't always—" and here she paused dramatically, slowly and deliberately letting her gaze sweep the room, "we don't always *reach out of the darkness!*"

I guess it was the word "darkness" that prompted Richard Farino to raise his hand and say, "No. We have to show Jesus's love to all people, even those whose skin is a different color from ours."

Then William Barton, Sister Lucy Joseph's prodigy, talked about how his family was shopping at Grandway the night before, and he held the door open for a black lady. Sister told him he was truly being a Jesus Christ in this world.

I yawned while other kids shot their hands in the air and the now-familiar litany began. God made us all. God loves us all. God does not discriminate against race. Everyone is equal. The black man is our brother.

At some point, though, my boredom started to change, slowly, like when a leaf begins to lose its color around the edges. I started thinking, really thinking about what everyone was saying. About loving people of different races. About being kind to others who are not like us. About not judging others on the basis of their skin color.

I thought about my wanting Danny to be invisible, my hoping no one would see him rocking in the car or hopping in the front yard, because his difference made me different. I remembered the day Tommy Donahue made fun of my brother and everybody laughed, the girl with the bad acne spraying me with the spittle of her glee. I thought about how kids glibly and thoughtlessly used the word *retard* to insult someone. I thought about how Danny couldn't help being Danny, just like our garbage man couldn't help having black skin.

I raised my hand.

"Yes, Ann," Sister Lucy Joseph nodded to me.

I stood up beside my desk, since that's what we had to do at Saint Anthony's when we asked or answered a question.

I took a deep breath and looked around the room at the faces of my classmates, people I had known for more than half my life.

"You talk about loving the black man," I began. "You say God wants us to love all people, regardless of how different from us they might be. And yet—" by now my voice was shaking, and I looked directly at Tommy Donahue. "And yet, when you see my brother, my retarded brother, you laugh at him, make fun of him, call him names. If you really believe God wants us to love everyone, doesn't that mean the retarded as well?"

I scanned the faces in the room. Some heads were bent, as if studying the desktops. Tom Donahue looked perplexed. John Koptula was fashioning a sling shot out of a rubber band, and Theresa Vitiello was writing a note to someone. The room was dead quiet, the loneliest silence I ever experienced in my life.

Sister Lucy Joseph stared at me long and hard, as if I had just said, "Jesus is not the Son of God."

"Sit down, Ann," she said.

My knees buckled. I gripped the desktop for support and slid into my seat.

"Okay, children," Sister Lucy Joseph said, distributing another set of dittoed sheets to us. On this page, in purple ink, were the words to the Reverend Martin Luther King's "I Have a Dream" speech. Sister asked us to recite the words aloud. Then, swallowing the bile gurgling in my throat, I sang—along with my peers—the lyrics to the Youngbloods' "Get Together," a pop ballad that urged us all to smile at and love one another.

Life with Runi 6

Aparna Das

Arunima (Runi) was born seven years after my third sibling. A fourth child born to a middle-class family in India is quite unusual, so everyone was surprised when my mother announced that she was pregnant. Runi certainly was an unplanned baby, but the excitement she brought into our lives was unmarred by the fact. She was as gorgeous as babies could get—jet-black, thick hair, and dark eyes that definitely looked at us!

The excitement of the first few months was short lived. Runi was suddenly very, very sick, with acute diarrhea, which was strange because our mother breastfed her initially. Hospitalization followed hospitalization, and it was finally ascertained that she was allergic to breast milk. Soy-milk formula was not as common in those days as it is now and had to be ordered from abroad. Injections, intravenous glucose drips to battle dehydration, strong medication, screams of pain from this tiny human being who really should not have to bear so much at such a young age (two to three months)—these are my overwhelming memories of the first few months of her life. She was getting epileptic seizures and was put on medication. Runi had developed an odd habit during her hospitalization. She would press both her palms to her temple and cross her legs together, applying immense pressure until she was fast asleep. If anyone disturbed this ritual, Runi would start crying hysterically—we learned this quickly. My siblings and I, ranging from ages seven to nine, supported each other as well as our mother, who was slowly crumbling under the pressure.

A letter in the mail brought news that we had been waiting for: my father had just been offered a job in Muscat, the capital of Oman. While a few months ago this would have been the best news possible, my parents received it with mixed feelings. On the one hand, it was obvious that the money would be very welcome. However, this would mean that my mother had to handle my sister's never-ending illness on her own. After much discussion though, the decision for him to go was made, and he left within six weeks of Runi's birth.

Runi finally came home after a total period of two months in the hospital. She required a great deal of care. The skin on her arms and legs was pitted with needle marks from endless prodding. While everyone wanted to help my mother, it seemed as if this ten-week-old baby could sense different arms when they tried to hold her. All we could do was watch while my mother, deprived of the much needed rest, held Runi for hours on end. We would help in other ways though—preparing her soybean formula, changing her diapers, and just sitting with our arms around our mother while she held little Runi. The pin pricks began fading away, and the care she was given began to take effect. Runi started accepting being held by us and actually seemed to enjoy it. She definitely recognized her siblings, and our attempts were rewarded by dazzling smiles and adorable giggles. It seemed almost miraculous that this wraith of a child was actually filling up and thriving. By the time Runi was six months old, even our mother had started looking more like herself again. Runi started putting on weight, was eating well, and had actually been transformed into a happy, bouncing baby. Life, everyone said, was looking up!

Fast forward to a year later when we joined our father in the Gulf. This was the beginning of Runi's endless crying spells, refusal to sleep in her crib, needing to be held almost through the night. I could see that my mother was reaching a breaking point. She was frustrated and depressed, and sleepless nights only added to these burdens. She felt she had to get out of the house and work if there were to be any way to preserve her sanity. We had also started attending afternoon shifts in an Indian school in Oman. Mum made an impulsive call to her sisters who had assured her of their support. Runi was sent away to one of my aunts who had the time and resources to give her the care she needed. Years seem to have fogged memories of the time that elapsed, but she was back soon enough since caring for Runi took more than anyone had bargained for. We were all thrilled to have our baby sister back, of course. Holding her during the night through the endless crying became normal again. A new habit Runi had developed was pooping in her pants and smearing it all over the kitchen. Wonderful! No matter how vigilant we were, Runi would find a way to get into the kitchen when we weren't looking and do her job. My other siblings and I would draw lots to see who would be stuck with the "enjoyable" job that day.

A helpful neighbor offered to baby sit her through the hours that we were in school and my mother got back from work. This too didn't work, and my mum finally quit that job. She stayed at home and things seemed to be working for a while, but nobody really understood the toll it was taking on my mother. The devastating results were to come soon, though.

A year down the line, all was no longer well on the professional front for our father. He was unhappy with the growing politics at his workplace and began to look for other options. It had also become somewhat of a pattern for Runi to go through troughs and peaks, and she was doing well, both physically and emotionally at this juncture. Both my parents decided to look for new jobs, and when this fell into place, we were required to come back to India to renew our visas. By this time, my mother, who had suspected all along that Runi was different from her other siblings, decided to visit a good pediatrician in India. He confirmed her misgivings that there was a developmental delay and that Runi would progress more slowly than other kids her age. My parents sat the three of us down and explained that our youngest sister would always require extra care. (Of course, this was twenty-five-odd years ago, and no one spoke to us about the benefits of intensive early intervention.) Our reactions were varied: Father not quite believing it, siblings not quite comprehending it, and Mother…well, Mother, sinking silently into a bog of depression. When we look back, everyone could see that she was unhappy, but this wasn't too different from how she had been since Runi's first trip to the hospital. She didn't discuss it with anyone else, and no one could have guessed what was to follow.

A few days later, our mother took an overdose of sleeping pills. The result was not an end to her misery as she had probably hoped, but severe brain damage that sentenced her to four years of a "vegetable" existence until she finally died.

That, of course, put paid to any plans we had of returning to the Gulf; we had to rebuild our lives in India. We were enrolled in a local school, and Runi was cared for by a stream of babysitters who stayed anywhere from between two weeks to a year. We were lucky with some that she took an immediate liking to, but heaven help anyone she disliked. Having developed no comprehensible language as yet though years had passed and she was now five, Runi would express her frustration by hitting out, pinching, and biting people around her. We would often go to school with scratches on our faces, necks, and hands, but if anyone asked— "the cat did it."

But with all these difficulties came many wonderful moments as well. Runi was becoming closer and closer to all of us, and people would often see her skipping along happily holding one of our hands. We didn't think twice about taking on "parenting" roles even as young kids while our father worked to make ends meet. It was taken for granted that we would come back from school and take over her care for the rest of the day. We'd spend time talking to her, singing to her (she *loved* songs and could listen for hours on end if possible), and taking her wherever we went. But the tantrums came regularly, too.

One night, we were all sitting and chatting in our bedroom. Runi was with us, probably twirling one of the small objects she was obsessed with and rocking back and forth as usual. Suddenly, we heard this beautiful, tuneful voice singing Kris Kristofferson's "Help Me Make It through the Night." It was Runi—who hadn't said one intelligible word all these years! She sang the whole song through. Our joy was beyond description, and we probably didn't sleep a wink just marveling at this much-needed miracle!

It wasn't as if the dam had burst and a river of speech and language was ready to flow. However, the year saw amazing development, and Runi was able to use words for simple communication. This was when an aunt from Australia visited us and was quite shocked to see that Runi was not going to school. She helped us do some research, and we were able to identify a special school that Runi started attending. The school was where Runi was diagnosed: we were finally given a name for something we had now been dealing with for six years. Runi started going to school and was placed in a classroom for children with different developmental issues. It was not easy. We had to get her ready for school—no mean task that! Breakfast time was always traumatic. Runi probably had sensory issues with some of the food that we were giving her, but we had no idea, of course. So there was force-feeding, spanking, pinching, retaliation, screaming—you name it. Each morning all of us left for our respective destinations completely frazzled and out of sorts. There were days when she would refuse to go to school, and her attendance was always quite patchy. On days that she did go, we would pick her up, often finding her completely disheveled and dirty, having spent the whole day in the sun because she would not sit in the classroom. One cannot be sure of the exact cause, but the irregular schooling, as well as the lack of any comprehensive Individualized Educational Plan for her, made things extremely difficult.

Runi had developed a few more obsessions by this time. One that has stayed to this day is her "fixation" for small objects. In those days, it was plastic animals. She would ask for a new packet every two weeks, reciting all the writing on the packaging over and over again until we finally gave in and bought her a new set. I bet the shopkeepers thought we were a strange family. We decided that we would use one shop for a few months, then move on to another one just to hide the fact that we were doing this so regularly. Finally after five shops had been tried, we came back to the first one again, hoping that the guy had forgotten. One look and he said, "Aren't you the people who keep buying those small animals!" Oh, the embarrassment! We were labeled for life!

Many gains were made through this time, though. We found out about an amazing special-education teacher who would take kids for one-on-one sessions during the week. Runi started attending two sessions per week, and this was perhaps the best period of her life. She loved her teacher, Rita, and she learned how to read and write and express herself using sentences. Rita used Runi's love for music and her obviously amazing memory as the basis of all her teaching. Runi progressed rapidly, and Rita's class was something that she truly looked forward to.

Our family maintained a sort of status quo for the next few years. Runi eventually stopped going to the special school and only attended her sessions with Rita. There were good days and bad. We learned to arrange our lives around Runi's needs. One of us would always be at home once the maid left for the day. We were growing up and our peer group became an important part of our lives. While we found we were not able to go out as much as everyone else did, all our friends knew Runi. Friends who wanted to get our attention would come and spend time with Runi, even bringing gifts like pens (another obsession), and, yes, *small animals* for her. She now was getting a packet of small animals sometimes as often as twice a week! Runi, in turn, could be extremely affectionate. All our visitors were greeted with bear hugs and would then be treated to a performance of songs, recitation of TV jingles, a run through of people's birthdays (Runi's phenomenal memory, again.) She is a wonderful mimic, and our guests were often in splits with her rendition of the gardener's strange accent or our grandaunt's funny walk.

It seemed only natural that I would pursue an honors degree in psychology and then a special-education course following my degree.

We have a close-knit family. One unspoken fear in each of our minds was "what if one of us leaves to work somewhere else or, heaven forbid, *gets married?*" We never discussed this among ourselves because it was such a worrying topic. My father believed that he would manage if he were the one left looking after Runi, but we couldn't imagine leaving him alone. "We're all in this together" was one thing we all believed. Nobody wanted to have to handle Runi alone—not just because she had some difficult behaviors but because one of us always needed to be around. We recently had a spate of pathetic house help and could not leave Runi alone with male cooks. To add to my own worries, I suspected that, now that I had done a special-education course and was working in the field, I would be the one handling Runi in the long term. While I felt responsible for her, I was wary of being taken for granted, guilty if I found myself spending too much time with my friends because it would mean that someone else had to sit at home. Looking back on those days, I am quite sure that *all* of us secretly nursed a combination of guilt, resentment, and a fear of being left in the lurch. One thing I was sure of was that Runi would, somehow or the other, be a part of my life. This was not because she was a "burden" I had to bear but because I couldn't feel comfortable any other way. And what did that mean in terms of marriage? Well, I had this optimistic hope that the person I would eventually spend my life with (if that person did exist) would be someone who would understand how I felt about my sister.

To my surprise such a person did exist. When I got married fifteen years ago, it was after feeling assured that my partner was a sensitive and caring person who would treat Runi with care. That was a hard period for all of us because I *did* go away. I did leave Runi. I did the unthinkable. My other siblings stayed with Dad for some time and then had to move on to look after their own jobs and futures. Runi moved back and forth between our homes for a few years, which was not the best arrangement, but it seemed unavoidable. The guilt and misery that would enter the lives of the people who she was not living with was hard to deal with. Runi also has this uncanny ability to internalize the moods of people around her, somewhat akin to the way an infant responds to its mother's mood. When things were going well for any of us, Runi would also become easier to handle. She was happy and willing to join in with day-to-day activities without a fuss. However, when the going got tough, it got even tougher. A few difficult years followed.

About four years after all this shuffling about, Runi moved more permanently into my home. My children were three-and-a-half years and one-year-old at that time. They came to know this "aunt" whom they were fond of because she was obviously important to their parents. It was hard to explain to them that, even though she looked so much bigger, they had to act more mature when she would not share things with them. Sometimes, after she had been particularly difficult, breaking objects around the house or lashing out at one of us, I would feel angry and resentful about being stuck with her. The guilt would come flooding back then, and I would remember that she was the one I used to feel so protective about at one point. It wasn't her fault that her brothers and sisters had gone on with their lives.

Happily though, Runi gave the kids their share of hugs and kisses too. It was always a pleasant surprise when she would come and pick them up if they fell and give them a "kiss to make it all better." They in turn learned that the world is made up of all kinds of minds, that it is okay to be different. Things went well for a few years.

Nothing lasts forever, though. About five years ago, Runi's behavior became almost impossible to handle. When she was in one of her moods, she would hurt herself and others around her and more or less wreck the house. Her tantrums could last for hours, and she would simply break anything in her path (including our video player once!), bite herself or others around her, lock herself in the bathroom, and turn all the taps on until the water ran out. It was very hard on everyone. Her epilepsy became worse than ever. My father and siblings pitched in by taking Runi to their houses to ease the pressure, but each house she went to was turned upside down—literally!

Many visits to neurologists and psychiatrists later, Runi was put on anti-anxiety and antidepression medication. This has made a difference.

I'd like to say "and they all lived happily ever after," but that is only the stuff that fairy tales are made of. What I can say with a great deal of confidence, though, is that the last twenty-nine-odd years have certainly given us food for thought. Runi has accepted us despite the way we are. It is the world that keeps trying to change her. Inclusion, in the true sense of the word, can only be achieved when we learn to live and let live. If her behavior is sometimes challenging to us, can we not give a thought to how frustrating we must be for her?

Many discussions, much advice from well-meaning friends and relatives, regrettable mistakes, a lot of laughter as well as some tears, and Runi continues to go through her ups and downs. I think I can say that she has more ups than downs. She is much calmer and enjoys doing little chores like taking in the washing, making her bed, and watering the plants in our garden. She can prepare her own breakfast and use the rice cooker to make her favorite *chaaval*. Asking questions is something that people with autism struggle with, but Runi has started asking simple questions, such as, "How many plates should I set on the table?" or " What color is this?" One set of sentences she repeats often— and in doing so, both asks and answers her own question—is "Why are you laughing? Because life is so funny." Once, we were walking down the road when Runi tripped over a rock. Now, she does not like surprises, and this accident could have upset her. I chose to ignore the little stumble, and we kept walking. Suddenly, Runi giggled.

"Why are you laughing?" I asked.

"Because life is so oops!!" she replied. Now that was original! She got the humor in the situation.

She is a beautiful child-woman today. Nearly thirty, she doesn't look a day older than fifteen. In many ways, she is like a little girl but shows flashes of maturity that make us wish we could unlock the secrets of her mind. There was a time when Runi and I had to fly from Bangalore to Delhi. The ground crew of this particular airline was shockingly ignorant. They refused to give us boarding passes because they were not sure that she was "fit to fly." I was angry, and things had started to get unpleasant. Having been questioned by at least two people and subjected to stares that made me feel uncomfortable, I refused to answer any more of their questions and demanded our passes. I know my voice had risen by then, too. Fortunately (for them), someone came and apologized and handed me the boarding passes. As I turned to take Runi through security, she may have noticed that I was a little shaken up and teary. She put her arm around me and said, "Didi (Hindi for older sister), are you okay?"

Yes, Runi, I am fine, and you are fine too. I love you just the way you are.

Autism Connects Us

7

Matthew K. Belmonte

Inching through Delhi's sclerotic early evening traffic on the way from Action for Autism in Jasola Vihar to the new metro station at Noida, I could either complain about taking an hour to travel the three kilometers or so across the river, or I could consider it an opportunity to reflect on the day, to learn something or to do something that I'm meant to do. This is what India is like: one learns to accept circumstance, on the presumption that if something isn't going according to plan, if something unforeseen is happening, there must be a reason for it. The cab ride, I reflect, is a lot like the past month and a half in this wondrous chaos of color and sound and people where untold stories intersect: in a place where one can move only so quickly, one may as well learn to make the most of the journey. And this notion of turning outrageous fortune into something of value is the frame within which I want to discuss autism and connectedness—connections within brains, within families, and within cultures.

* * *

India is thick with people and things. I had to get used to being touched, used as a handhold or a tool by strangers dodging through crowds. It took a few tries at queueing before I learned to stand close enough to the person in front of me to prevent others from inserting themselves in the gap. The most charming aspect of this lack of physical personal distance is that it comes with a corresponding lack of *social* distance: if I were to walk into one of my old haunts—say, the 1369 Coffee House in Cambridge, Massachusetts, or the CB2 Café in Cambridge, England—sit down at a table with people whom I didn't know, and begin asking questions about their families, their jobs, their salaries, I would be uncouth. If I were to walk into the Indian Coffee House in Kolkata and do the same, I would be normal. Once you've experienced this way of doing things and got comfortable with it, you realize how much easier it makes life—especially if, like me and like a lot of first-degree relatives of people with autism, you've never actually been able to figure out social approach. In India, there is no expectation of privacy in public places and no assumption that people would want privacy in a public place; one, therefore, can dispense with most of the subtle—and, for me, error-prone—social signaling that goes into establishing an invitation into someone else's space. Everyone here remarks on how quickly I seem to have adapted to a foreign culture, and I suppose that this is because, in a way, I'm in a foreign culture every day. At least here in India I've been told the rules explicitly, and have only to follow them.

It's as though there's an activation energy to social interaction: like molecules in a pressure chamber, we run into each other but tend to bounce off. Only if we happen to approach closely, to notice something about one another, do we actually bond. Reducing the extent of personal space, physically and socially, is like cranking up the pressure in a reaction vessel or like adding a catalyst: when we're forced to see and to know that much more of each other, there's a better chance that we'll stick. Psychologist Yaacov Trope has studied this correspondence between physical perceptual distance and social cognitive distance, and psychologist

Richard Nisbett has theorized on the ways in which cultures that are either holistic and unifying (as in Asia) or analytic and divisive (as in Europe and North America) exert corresponding effects on the cognitive styles of individual people within these cultures. I find that these ideas are much on my mind here: perhaps India's lack of social distance and its emphasis on perception of the whole rather than analysis into parts could compensate, in part, for autistic cognitive biases that emphasize things over people and details over gestalts. In other words, being autistic in India might not be as rough as it is elsewhere because cultural and social structures could provide more support and scaffolding.

I can see this emphasis on people rather than parts even in the way the taxi drivers operate: trying to reach my hotel, I made the mistake of handing the taxi driver a map of Delhi that pinpointed our exact location and the exact location of the hotel, and highlighted the route between. He put the map aside, started driving, and every few minutes shouted out the window to ask directions and landmarks. He wasn't thinking of the route as a progress through the space defined by the map. He was thinking of the route as a sequence of actions in relation to neighborhoods and landmarks that people could tell him about. Autistic people tend to be good with maps and poor with people, and this is the most *non*autistic culture that I've ever experienced. Although this emphasis on people makes India more difficult for me in minor ways—such as dealing with the taxi drivers!—in a broader sense, it creates a supporting structure, akin to what Russian developmental psychologist Lev Vygotsky called a *scaffold*. Those of us who may need extra help navigating social interactions don't have to work quite as hard to meet the social world halfway because it works harder to meet us.

People with Asperger syndrome especially, I've remarked to my Indian colleagues, must have an easier time of it here. Asperger syndrome and other relatively mild variants are in a way the most frustrating forms of autism-spectrum conditions: those with Asperger syndrome have all (and in many cases more) of the speech and language skills that others have, yet applying these skills to social communication and its subtle and rapid signaling is what flummoxes them. Put them in an environment where there is less ambiguity, where social roles are more prescribed, where the questions are more scripted ("Tell me about your family?" "What's your job?" "What's your salary?"), and they're in their element. Here, in India, even romantic relationships are arranged, with the options presented to each other one by one. There is an algorithm: all parties know what's on the agenda, and there is no shame or embarrassment to it. It's this algorithmic aspect to social interaction that the West has lost, as traditional gender roles have been dismantled. This isn't at all to say that the loss of these constraining roles is a bad thing! The only trouble is, at least in the West, there's been no structure to replace them. My father felt quite at home coming of age in the 1950s because he had a script with prescribed roles: he could tell what was expected of him, and he knew what to expect of the people with whom he worked or those he loved. Not so today.

If India has this mollifying effect on social anxiety, its effect on work anxiety is no less (leaving aside, in this context, all the horror stories about its competitive schools and exams). Like a lot of relatives of people with autism, I have what a psychologist would call high "trait anxiety." If something's on the agenda, I can't stop thinking about it until it's done. If I have an appointment, I have to get there on time. I latch onto every detail; then I don't let go until it has been crossed off the list. Put me in a situation where circumstances call for this sort of behavior, an atmosphere of deadlines and pressures and exactly timed schedules, and this high trait anxiety becomes high "state anxiety": I'm perpetually on edge. A little of this is actually productive, but day in, day out, and it begins to make of me a nervous wreck. Academic science in the U.S. and the U.K. is an anxiety-laden proposition: there's always a deadline for a manuscript, a grant proposal, a conference submission. Everything has to be done today, or better yesterday. If you miss the deadline, you miss out on the publication, the grant money, the visibility. This go-go-go atmosphere doesn't mix well with a person who dwells on every detail until it's complete and only then moves on. It's the multitasking that kills me. In India, though, one can forget about getting things done today, because it isn't going to happen. Getting something done will require filling in at least ten separate forms and submitting them to at least five separate bureaucracies. (Remember, these people learned the art of bureaucratization from the British Empire!) Because traveling to an appointment requires navigating these choked streets, one can never be certain what time a meeting is going to happen, and one ought never to plan for more than a couple of occasions in any single day. This paralysis brings on a degree of calm acceptance: when you can't do what you want, you do what you can—and at the end of the day, you relax and you don't worry.

When I contemplate this hidden benefit of paralysis, I can't help but think of my father again. It was June 1992 when I first saw his Parkinson's disease coming on, while he and I were driving across North America to deliver me to graduate school in San Diego. Never one to submit to chance and spontaneity, my father had planned and reserved an elaborate series of motels at intervals along a well-specified route. (Interesting road sign or billboard? Want to stop and take in a museum or a natural park? Too bad, no time, we have a reservation, and we have to be in middle-of-nowhere New Mexico by nightfall.) The motel somewhere west of Las Cruces was wrapped in a desert twilight that I had never before witnessed. I wanted to walk through it to a mesa that rose in the desert close by. My father insisted on coming along. But he was shuffling, couldn't seem to lift his feet from the ground. "Why don't you go back to the room, and I'll see you there," I suggested. "I'll follow you anywhere," he shot back. I couldn't bear his struggle. I abandoned the mesa, and we turned back to the motel bar's neon and plastic predictability.

My father's problem, always, had been that he tried too hard, couldn't ever let go of things. He held on to slights and insults from decades ago, as strongly as he remembered acts of kindness and friendship. He was a loyal, genuine man, albeit not a forgiving one. When he liked you, you knew it was real. When he disliked you, there was no redemption. My father's way of making sense of the world was to draw boundaries: good and bad, desirable and undesirable, friends and enemies. He partitioned his universe into manageable chunks and details and tried to understand it one piece at a time—and in this analytical habit my father and I are much alike. Parkinsonism did for him what all his years of living could not do: it gave him the ability to accept circumstance and to allow events to flow around and through him. When you can no longer bend your world to your will, when you lose even the ability to control your own body, your own speech, your own *bladder*, you learn to stop trying so hard all the time and to experience the world without any effort to control it. As the taxi bobs in this slow current of Amrapali Marg and the Yamuna River flows under us in the winter evening's low sunlight, I think of bathing in the Mandakini River a few weeks ago, floating, without trying to swim.

My mother raised an autistic son in the "dark ages" of the 1960s, when Bruno Bettelheim's dominant psychoanalytical theory framed autistic behavior as a reaction to frigid parenting. I can only imagine what it must have been like for her to have been asked by a physician—a supposed authority whom we were meant to trust—"Mrs. Belmonte, don't you feel *guilty*?" (Yes, this actually happened.) As we now know, from my work and that of others on the neurophysiology of autistic perception, Bettelheim got one thing—and *only* one thing—right: autistic behavior *is* a reaction to rejection. Rather than rejection by the mother, though, it's a rejection mediated by one's own nervous system, by a brain that makes sensory experiences so intense as to become unbearable. Faced with all the world's sound and fury unmediated and unfiltered, autistic withdrawal from contact becomes understandable as a survival strategy. To her credit, Mum never believed a word of Bettelheim's dogma. But her story of the early days, and my own experience as I grew up with my brother, watching the white-coated parade of fools with their special diets and medicines and experimental shots in the dark, did instill a skepticism of medical and scientific authority. Even now, when I have the qualifications of a scientist, I feel that for the past two decades I've been on something of a masquerade: like my father, I draw boundaries, and in the autism world, there have been two camps: families, and researchers. I often feel like a double agent. I was once told, as a postgraduate, by a scientist whom I respected, that my status as a family member compromised my objectivity. I would like to think that, although my personal experiences inform my hypotheses, I test those hypotheses just as rigorously as any other scientist would do. On the other hand, I don't *feel* like a professional scientist: I am in this game not to garner grants or to build my name or to make a career: I just want the problem solved. I don't really give a damn who solves it.

Because I had nothing to compare it to, I actually thought that my family was normal. I remember walking home from primary school to the little house that my father had bought before I was born, a *thud - thud - thud* emanating from the room in the back corner. It was my brother's head against his bedroom wall. My mother would be up there trying to restrain him, to keep him from hurting himself, and as soon as the bus carried my father back from his office, he would join her. In the United States in those days, before legislation mandated an appropriate education for all children with disabilities, no school would take my brother. So Mum had built a Montessori classroom in the basement and was spending her days with him there. After my brother calmed down, my father would cast off his tie, fetch his martini mix out of the freezer, and sink into a numb stupor in front of Walter Cronkite, Gerald Ford, and the aftermath of the Vietnam War. "Stupid," he would mutter at the war. He had met my mother in Southeast Asia, where they both were in the diplomatic corps, before, he said, the whole place went to hell. At the supper table, if one said the wrong thing, looked at him the wrong way, he would fly into a rage. What was he angry with? Life. It had let him down. He knew what he wanted to do, and none of this, none of all this activity revolving round my brother's autism, was part of that script. When my brother was diagnosed, white-coated professionals advised my parents to place him in an institution—in those days, these were institutions for the mentally retarded, who weren't differentiated from the autistic—and to forget him and move on. Otherwise, they warned, "he will destroy your family." My parents, of course, couldn't listen to that heartless advice. My father used to reminisce about their wedding, and I have always remembered that when he swore "till death do us part" he choked, recognizing the significance of the words. He loved my mother deeply. His rage at her, and at me and my sister and my brother, really was anger at the circumstance that was preventing him from giving us all that he wanted to give, in the way he wanted to give it.

A couple of years later, I was eight years old and we had just moved house, into a bigger (and, in my father's valuation, therefore better) place in one of those sterile suburban neighborhoods carved out by bulldozers. The house was a trophy, an image of success. I missed the old neighborhood, where there were people. I walked home from school and opened the door to my mother's sobs. (My brother was calm and occupying himself in his room.) This wasn't an unusual event. I would always ask, "What's wrong? How can I help." Of course, there never was any way, really, that I could help, aside from offering an ineffectual hug or condolence. I had learned to feel as powerless as my mother must have felt. Sometimes I worked off the frustration by vandalizing the half-completed McMansions on the next street over, kicking the shit out of their particle-board walls. There were a golden couple of hours between the time I arrived back from school and the time my father arrived back from the office, an interlude when Mum and I could talk. She was collapsed against the banister halfway to the upstairs landing. (It was one of those faux banisters, processed in some factory from wood chips or something, an image of affluence uprooted from its referent.) The autumn's late afternoon sun spilled across my mother's bedroom and onto the deep-red pile carpet. She began telling me how my father wasn't the man that she had married. I don't recall the specifics of the rest of the spiel because, to me, it was all part of a script that I had seen coming. I could understand this; in school, I had peers ("friends," I used to call them, though they weren't) whose parents were divorced. It would be a resolution, at least, an end to this ceaseless buffeting. The next afternoon, though, my mother backtracked: all those things that she had said about my father, that didn't mean that she and he were going to split up. "Oh," I nodded. Many years later, when I was back on a break from graduate school and Mum and I were walking in a nearby park, I brought up this episode, and she told me that on that day she had chosen a flat and was ready to move us into it—but at the last moment, she felt that she had to stay, for my sake. I stopped in my tracks. For *my* sake?! "Mum," I gasped, nineteen years on, "what the fuck were you thinking?!"

Amid this turmoil, science was my refuge and my stability. I was always uncomfortable with any situation in which there was more than one right answer. I didn't want the responsibility of defining my universe; I wanted to discover what had already been laid out for me. Science was my mother who would make all the choices for me and keep me safe from the chaos of people and sensations outside its walls. In this respect, I was very similar to my older brother. Neither of us could tolerate not being in control of our surroundings. We wanted some master plan, some canon that would tell everything and everyone how to behave. We were poorly disposed toward change because it's so much more difficult to make sense of one's environment when it keeps slipping out of one's analysis. Things precarious or capricious—a newspaper hanging off the edge of the coffee table, furniture arranged at arbitrary angles instead of rectilinearly, items not stacked or lined up in order of decreasing size—were abhorrent to us. The only solution in such a case was to attempt to correct the irregularity or, if that were impossible, to leave the room and to try to deny its existence. In contrast, regular, repetitive events—the rise and fall of shadows under street lights, the rhythm of a twig caught in a bicycle wheel, water flowing in systems of pipes—were comforting because they gave us the power of prediction and control. As we both grew older, we diverged; this preoccupation with order began to dictate my behavior less rigidly. I could speak and converse; he could not. I began to learn pragmatism and to accommodate wills and actions external to myself. I was still very shy with strangers, though, because people, especially people with whom one has no experience, are by far the most unpredictable elements of the universe and the greatest threat to one's own control of it. In the back of my mind always was the similarity in the ways in which my brother and I dealt with the world. I was a scientist. He was autistic. At times, it became difficult, at least qualitatively, to tell the difference. I could so easily have turned out as he, or he I.

Fascinated with the difference and similarity between siblings with and without autism, I had always wanted to study pairs like my brother and me. In 2002, I wrote a proposal for a grant from Cure Autism Now to do exactly that, as a postdoctoral scientist with Simon Baron-Cohen at Cambridge: we would do brain scans on children with autism-spectrum conditions and on their nonautistic siblings and compare these to unrelated children without any autism in the family. One day in 2003, a mother from north London rang up and said that she had two boys who wanted to participate—there was just one thing: they were identical twins; was that okay? I nearly fell off my chair. Here was a chance to study how development of the autistic brain and mind might diverge in two people who shared exactly the same genome. When I visited for a diagnostic interview, I found two very different boys, though with some curious similarities. L., the one who hadn't been breathing when he was born, was certainly on the autism spectrum: he met criteria for social impairment, language delay, and ritualistic behaviors. His brother M., though, seemed much more functional: he met the criterion only for rituals but not for language or social impairment. The scans, too, showed great differences in the structures and functions of their brains: L. had a typically autistic enlarged frontal lobe and a small cerebellum and only isolated spots of brain activity in relation to the problem-solving task that I had set for the brothers. M.'s brain structure was more the norm, and his brain activity showed many separate parts of cortex coming together to solve a complex cognitive problem.

L. and M. had a tight bond with each other. Even before they began speaking English, they'd developed their own private language. L. was lost in the fast-moving social milieu of school, but M. could understand both his brother L. and their peers, and stepped in as a sort of social translator. I felt that I knew a little bit about what M. was doing because, in a less literal sense, I too could speak my brother's language: I understood the comfort that he felt in regularity and predictability because I felt it also—our parents didn't get it, our sister didn't get it; but my brother and I, we got it. I marveled at these two very unique human beings, L. and M., who had emerged from one and the same set of genetic instructions. If the path toward autism could diverge so easily and yet leave such similarity, even with the same genes, then might it be possible to steer development toward an outcome like that of

M., who's able to glimpse what a person with autism sees but also able easily to communicate those insights to the rest of us? And if this is the breadth of potential from a single set of genes, what of siblings who share, on average, only half their genes?

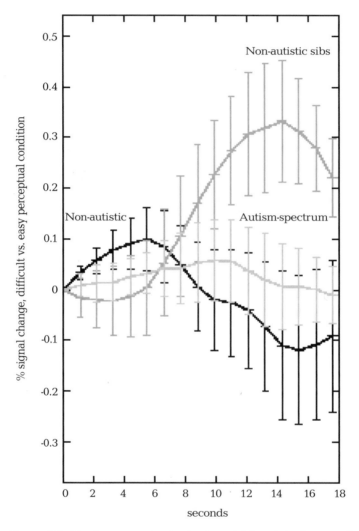

Figure 7.1: Blood oxygenation in the frontal lobe of the brain in boys with autism spectrum conditions (ASC), their non-ASC brothers, and unrelated typically developing children who are solving a difficult cognitive problem

Source: Reprinted with permission from Belmonte et al. (2010) *Journal of Child Psychology and Psychiatry 51*, 259–276, published by Blackwell Publishing on behalf of the Association for Child and Adolescent Mental Health.

In Figure 7.1 the unrelated non-ASC boys (black line) rapidly switch on the frontal cortex, then switch it off when it's no longer needed. The ASC boys (light grey line) don't fully switch it on until after the time allowed for the problem has expired. The non-ASC brothers (darker grey line) also take a long while to switch on, but when they do they drive brain activation to an abnormally high amplitude. Is this intensity what rescues them from autism?

Graphs of brain activity show just how fine a line separates autistic and nonautistic siblings: when we ask these children to go from solving an easy problem to solving a difficult one, their frontal lobes "switch on" to meet the increased demand. For children in families unaffected by autism, this peak of activity happens early, near the left end of the time axis: they quickly ramp up brain response when confronted with a difficult problem, then just as quickly switch it off when the problem has been solved. Autistic children don't show the peak until several seconds later—too late, in fact, for the added brain activity to be of any use in solving this timed problem and very much consonant with what people with autism express about the world moving too quickly for them to be able to jump in and interact with it. Most interesting to me, though, is the plot for the nonautistic siblings: they (or should I say "we"?) manifest the same remarkable delay, with the brain response coming too late to be of use in behavior. When this delayed peak of activity does come, though, it's a much greater increase even than that of the unrelated nonautistic children: although we seem to take forever to press the accelerator, when we finally do press it, we put the pedal to the metal. Could it be that this is what has rescued us—that we're resistant to autism because we're doing something differently when switching on our brains? Or is this difference in our brains more a consequence than a cause of our being nonautistic? When I see the graph, I think of my father and his habit of trying too hard. There it is, on paper: even when it's futile, when it's too late to be of any use or influence on the outcome, the nonautistic siblings (and, I'm guessing, the parents, too) keep hammering at the problem, not content to accept circumstance.

My father, of course, had a script to follow: overcome anti-immigrant prejudice, enter the educated class, start a career, fall in love and marry, raise heirs to what he had built. Autism disrupted that script. Though my father worked incessantly for my brother, to make certain that he had the services and opportunities that he needed, it was clear that the life story that he had imagined for himself was a very different one. As a child of Italian immigrants, my father identified with a culture that placed disproportionate value on sons and on the eldest son, in particular. My brother was that eldest son, and when he couldn't fill the envisioned role, the duty fell to me. The same traits that made me identify with my brother—the single-mindedness, the persistence, the narrowness of focus and preoccupation with getting every detail right—convinced my parents that I was not at all like him: I had drive and potential, while he had a neurological disease. Any achievement of mine seemed of value not so much in itself, or for me, but for how it reflected on the people and institutions around me. All the science prizes, the computer-programming internship, the university admissions, even my exam scores, these became items of conversation, bragging rights. My father, of course, could not separate his pride in me from his pride in himself—or, I think, his genuine love for me from his love for himself. He spoke incessantly of how well off I was going to be when I got a highly paid job "in my field" of computer science. By the time I had finished university, I had grown weary of being a trophy, not so much a son but a display-case item. I wanted to hit back, to destroy something that was of value to him. And, of course, the thing that was of greatest value to him was me. So I sabotaged it. I announced that I wasn't going to look for a computing job, at all. I had added a major in English literature, and I ploughed further into it, throwing myself into writing and theater projects and drifting away from computers.

At the same time, though, what drew me to literature was the same fascination that had drawn me into computing: I was interested in the process of representation, in how meaning could be encapsulated within a system. At some level, it didn't matter whether that system were a literary text in which meaning had been distilled into recognizable character archetypes and plot scripts or a computer program in which meaning had been loaded into symbolic data and algorithms. I was fascinated with the very old and the very recent; I specialized both in Anglo-Saxon and in modern literature. Anglo-Saxon attracted me because it was all about boundaries: the walls of the mead-hall separating warmth and life from the winter and death outside, the kingdom beset from without by invaders and from within by a gnawing conflict between Germanic and Christian heroic ideals—all this seemed visible not only in the stories but in the very language, its syntax and sound. Likewise, modern literature attracted me because it represented the awakening of the narrator, a self-consciousness of the act of storytelling and the process of representation.

The psychoanalyst and literary critic Jacques Lacan wrote, "Le symbole se manifeste d'abord comme meurtre de la chose"—the symbol manifests firstly as the killing of the thing—and I was quite conscious of the fact that these abstractions that I had been analyzing or creating, whether in the form of computer programs or of narratives, were separate from veridical reality. The veridical *thing*, as distinct from the abstract *symbol*, is what was salient to me and to my brother: where others perceived the *thing* as an instance of some category, we saw the details first (he much more than I) and then built up the abstractions that these details evoked, effortfully and deliberately. This very effort, though, made me more conscious of the process of representation. I was constantly bothered and uncomfortable with the gulf between symbol and referent, and, as literature had taught me, a narrator who is more conscious of the effort of narration can, almost paradoxically, in the end achieve a more genuine and fundamental understanding of the characters and events surrounding him or her, precisely because (s)he is so impaired at automatic social perception and must concentrate harder to construct an explicit theory of reality, to piece a story together from perceptual fragments. As I was to learn some years later, this *narrative* disconnection in the autistic mind maps onto *neural* disconnections in the autistic brain: instead of coordinating many separate parts of the brain in a complex narrative, each part of the brain plays its own scene or vignette in isolation from the others, and a story becomes more an unordered scrapbook of sights and sounds and textures. This lack of coordination makes it much more difficult for people with autism to make sense of the story because, instead of representing it as a small set of instances of archetypes, motifs, or tropes, they must represent a large collection of veridical percepts, unintegrated with each other. It's as though I were to gaze at the scene outside my window and instead of immediately understanding "window" as a category, I would have to understand each pane and each muntin, then build atop these the idea of "window." All this effort at everyday representation imposes a huge cognitive load, which can overwhelm. If—and this is a big "if"—the individual can manage this cognitive load, though, the result is a deeper understanding of reality, one that explicitly roots and situates abstract symbols and categories in their veridical referents. This induction of category or symbol from referential roots is the way all narrative representation, and mental representation in general, proceeds; the big difference in autism is that this process is deliberate and explicit rather than automatized and is, therefore, open to analysis. In literature, then, just as in science, understanding autism helps us to understand humanity.

Although some of the differences between my brother and me were categorical—I could speak and he couldn't—others were a matter of degrees: we both had trouble with loud sounds, were fascinated by sensory patterns, lined up our toys in order of size or color, had a nervous habit of hand-flapping, couldn't immediately recognize new faces, felt anxious looking into others' eyes, spoke too softly or too loudly, and shied away from flexible social interaction. And sometimes even those distinctions that might seem categorical really are just matters of degree, when one considers the motivation behind them: my brother got his predictability fix from sifting sand or rocking his head back and forth, and I got mine from programming computers and poring over science books, but these respective habits of ours reflected, fundamentally, the same fascination with order and control. So, I was interested not only in the differences between autistic and nonautistic brains but also in the similarities between those brains as a function of degrees of autistic traits. The peaks that I described in the graph are averages: every brain is different; some look more "autistic" (in terms of delayed timing of activation), and some look less "autistic." Trying to sort out how this "autisticness" of brain activity might go along with degrees of "autisticness" in behavior and personality, I built a mathematical function that would measure just how delayed each individual's brain activity was. It was no great surprise that, in the autism-spectrum group, this degree of autisticness of brain function correlated with the degree of autistic behavior. It perhaps also came as no great surprise that the same correlation obtained in the nonautistic siblings. What may have been more surprising, though, is my finding that this relationship between delayed brain activation and slightly "autistic" ways of thinking also held in the unrelated, nonautistic children. When we look at autism, we really are looking at a basis of human cognitive diversity—a realization that may help us understand why autism exists, not only biologically but also teleologically.

I've written elsewhere that people with autism are "human, but more so": the genetic risk for autism is accumulated from a huge number of genes—probably in the hundreds—each of which confers a very small effect and each of which contributes not only to autism but to human cognitive diversity in general. Many of these autism genetic risk factors are quite common, and some of them actually are the major alleles—that is, the autism-associated version of the gene is the one that's carried by most people. It's a lot like skin color: the trait is genetically mediated, but there are so many genes that participate in determining pigmentation and so many different ways in which these genes can be altered that we have a beautiful array of human diversity—really not anything that we would want to have any other way.

In terms of behavior, too, when we look at autism, we are seeing ourselves: my father's and my own analytical habit of chopping up the world into manageable categories is a common mode of thought, and when one considers it, there actually isn't much distance between our abstract categorization and the more concrete categories implemented by an autistic child who lines up toys in order of height or color. We correctly label people autistic when such rituals—lining up toys, flipping light switches, rearranging furniture, repeating words or sounds in memorized sequences—displace flexible social communication; but, on the other hand, isn't this sort of ritual speech and action all that any of us do at a wedding or a funeral or, for that matter, every morning when we wake up and brush our teeth the same way? There is a comfort, an abdication of narrative responsibility in having a script—any script—and this is what modernity has shown us. As Thomas Pynchon's famous antihero Tyrone Slothrop observed, with a hint of irony, either we're here for some reason, or we're just here, and we actually would prefer to have some reason, any reason.

Even—and perhaps especially—after raising an autistic son in those cold days of the 1960s and 1970s, my mother still believes that events happen for a reason. I tend to agree: even if it may be up to us to figure out what that reason might be, or actually to construct it after the fact, it helps to know that events are directed toward a purpose, that there is some deep teleology that we may not now be able to discern. Perhaps there is no reason other than the rationale that we ourselves may construct post hoc. This very faith, though, is what keeps us up to the nearly superhuman task of constructing purpose and, thus, fulfills itself. It's this notion of self-fulfilling faith that brings me back to my taxi ride through Delhi. In a culture that swings toward holism rather than analysis, families rather than individuals, and the tapestry rather than the threads, it's impossible to avoid a sense of fatalism and synchronicity: nothing happens by accident. Am I delayed because I was meant to have some time to contemplate this essay? Does my brother have autism because he was meant to show us something about humanity—perhaps to show me something that I can show you?

My Brother's Speaker   8

Debra L. Eder

My brother Steven is a fifty-year-old man who has never spoken a word. I grew up with him, and we have never had a conversation. He sing-songs sounds, patterns of meaningless echolalia:

> "Ah de chuck a lay.
> Ah de chuck a lay.
> Leh coco lie.
> Leh coco lie.
> Leh coco lie.
> Ah. Ehhhh.
> Ah. Ehhhh.
> Ah. Ehhhh."

What can I say about living with a nonverbal autistic brother? I spent the first seventeen years of my life surviving with Steven. As a child, I did not think of his invasiveness as a relationship. It was difficult to experience his behavior as a form of communication.

19 Elmwood Avenue:
Debbie's house, 1968–72

19 Elmwood Avenue, a four-bedroom house, sits on a half-acre lot in West Long Branch, New Jersey. There are seven of us in the family—four girls and Steven. The order of the siblings, which spans nine years, is Liz, Steven, Debbie, Melissa, and Nancy. Steven is eighteen months older than me. I'll share a room with Liz until I'm thirteen and she goes off to college. The "babies," Melissa and Nancy, share a room. They're eleven months apart and as close as twins.

Nightmare and morning

Blue bathroom. Debbie and Liz's bedroom

I stand at the blue bathroom window. It's dark outside. But I don't turn on the lights because I know that people can see inside lit houses. 19 Elmwood Avenue is a one-story ranch, a horror story, and I'm going to escape by jumping out the window, then climbing over the fence in the back yard. There are a lot of flaws in my plan. I'm barefoot and wearing a long, flannel nightgown. This bathroom is in Daddy and Mommy's bedroom, and Mommy could wake up. Daddy might come to bed from the family room where he's watching TV and drimmel-dozing on his La-Z-Boy recliner. The yellow bathroom down the hall is a better route, but it stinks from Steven's doody.

I raise the window sash, hike the gown to my thighs, then sit, straddling the ledge like a balance beam to swing my legs over so it won't be too far to the ground to drop down.

Dream disrupted. The ceiling light beams like a searchlight into my eyes. The radio blasts in the kitchen: "WABC. Dan Ingram! Go! Go! Go! Go! Go!" My blanket is yanked off. I grumble awake from my usual dream of escape. My legs shiver. Steven hulks at the foot of my bed. I stretch forward but don't get up, flail to grab the covers, and shout, "Leave me alone, Steven! Get out of here!"

Steven repeats these actions every morning, and I react the same way. It gets a rise out of me, but I do not think of it as an older brother's teasing. His actions are repeated every day yet feel random, without meaning, as if they are controlling him, not that he controls them.

Steven is all action and no narrative.

* * *

Autism was uncommon in the 1960s and 1970s. Today, the diagnosis is more prevalent. There is far greater awareness—someone knowing someone who has an autistic child—as well as representation in popular culture, from CNN to Yahoo. The siblings of autistic people stay in the background.

When I was growing up, resources were limited. Still, my parents did not give up on Steven. They helped found programs for the autistic where Steven could get services. I don't believe they ever accepted how unteachable he is.

Steven could not be taught the most basic skills. My parents had to bathe him, and he has never learned how to take care of himself. I don't blame my parents for not institutionalizing Steven. There was no suitable facility, and the option was unthinkable. Steven was their child and one of the family. He is my brother.

Hide and stalk

Nine-year-old Debbie: Mommy and Daddy's
bedroom. Steven's bedroom

After school, I hide behind a coat in the hall closet, wrap its sleeves around me and hug myself. It's not safe here; Steven could find me when he comes home from the Search Activities Center. I dash for Mommy and Daddy's room, which is the farthest from the front door. I'm going to hide in Mommy's closet; but before I do, I peek into Daddy's closet like a secret diary. I never hide in Daddy's closet, but today I touch the sleeves of his suit jackets. This comforts me. Daddy wears the same drip-dry suit for an entire week. He has one in popsicle blue. Another is chocolate brown. I'm curious about a shiny orange shoe-box-size carton of "Trojan Premium Latex condoms" on the top shelf.

Sometimes Daddy yells; if I'm the one he's angry at, I'll hide from him, so he doesn't spank me. Or I'll run away from him with books in my pants. I don't have to worry about that now because Daddy is at his dental office and won't be home until dinner. Besides I'm more scared of his yelling than his spanking, which, if he catches me, is only a potch on the tuchus.

"Ah. Ehhhh. Ah. Ehhhh. Ah. Ehhhh." Steven is in the house! I duck into Mommy's closet, which is narrow but deep so I burrow toward the back. I stand still and listen. I hunch down near the shoes, and I listen. Where is Steven? He likes to roam around the house. I'm not sure if he's searching for me. Steven doesn't know enough to open up closet doors to find me, but I'm trapped. I'd like to go and lie in bed and read, but I never read in my bedroom during the day. It's the most obvious place if he's looking for me. What do I do? If I leave the closet, he could stumble upon me. I am trapped if he's looking for me and trapped if he finds me as he ambles through the house! I'm trapped while hiding and trapped in the open. What would Nancy Drew do? I want to read but where? The family room is too far. It's never quiet in the "babies'" bedroom; Melissa and Nancy are always playing together in there. Besides, Steven might be crobbling them. Should I read in Steven's bedroom? Should I chance it? And even if Steven goes to his room, he might not crobble me. He could just try to get me to play his turntable. I hate it when he crobbles me—touching my face, grabbing my arm, my shoulder. I wish he were a normal brother. If only he would just talk! Why can't he just say what he has to say or leave me alone?

Steven's room is closest to Mommy and Daddy's room, down a short hallway. I tiptoe past the blue bathroom. I don't close the door to his bedroom because it's never closed. He won't see me if I stand near the walls with the book shelves. The shelves are full of books. There's a whole collection of Hardy Boys, which I ignore. I won't risk crossing the hall to snatch a Nancy Drew book from my bedroom. One unsolved mystery: why are there so many books in Steven's room? Steven cannot read them. He doesn't even know his ABC's, and I learned to read before kindergarten.

I select the "F" of the Golden Book encyclopedia. It's my favorite with its cartoon-like drawings of food that remind me of the sandwiches Dagwood eats in the Blondie comic strip. This moment of choosing calms me a little. I cringe-curl at the foot of Steven's bed and hide in the book.

* * *

19 Elmwood Avenue. There were walls partitioning off rooms but no shelter.

Living, family, dining, bed, and bath—colored with hope, these words shape a space that evokes home—rooms filled with harmony for the people who inhabit them.

Struggling to write this, I look up *living* and *family* in the dictionary. There are contradictory definitions; I try to select the most optimistic. I imagine a reader who is seeking comfort and understanding. She could be Debbie.

Living as a verb means "to exist and endure" but can also express "to experience or enjoy life to the full." And, at its best, *family* is "two or more people who share goals and values, have long-term commitments to one another, and reside usually in the same dwelling place."

Growing up, I lived a solid, middle-class lifestyle in a house with a family. My material needs were well met. I had more than enough to eat; we often ate steaks, veal chops, and lamb chops, seasoned with garlic salt. My mother was not a good or attentive cook. She put the meat in the oven, and it was considered ready when my father came home from work. He was often late, and the meat was overdone.

I did not wear hand-me-downs. I slept in my own bed. But when I took a shower in the morning, Steven was turning the knob on the bathroom door. The bathroom door was the only door we were allowed to lock.

I was not deprived of books. I could buy as many books as I wanted through the school book club. I had "all the comforts of home" without being comforted. Books were how I survived.

Stand-off in the family room

Twelve-year-old Debbie: Kitchen and family room

Where is everyone? Steven's not home yet. Liz isn't home, as usual. She's either at color guard or hanging out with her cool girlfriends, Patty and Joy, or with Freddie. She stays out so late with him that she has been missing her curfew a lot lately. I wonder if I'll have a boyfriend one day. Melissa and Nancy have each other; they aren't around anyway, even if I wanted to play with them; Daddy's at work; Mommy's probably taking one of her classes at Monmouth College. Steven's not home yet. The coast is clear.

I just finished eating my rice; now I get to read! The bottom of the pot is black and crusty where the kernels burnt. But the rice was sticky soft and yummy buttery the way I like to eat it every day after school. I'm going to leave the pot in the sink and go and read on Daddy's La-Z-Boy recliner. That's not selfish. I ate the rice out of the pot, so there's no plate to wash. I hate it when Mommy calls me selfish. I should reward myself. I'm done with my homework, which was super fast as usual. I get good grades without having to study hard. I'm not going to wash the pot. Anyway, Mommy says I'm the most like her of all of her children because I'm so sensitive. If I don't wash the pot, it's because I take after her. I didn't stir the rice, and her spaghetti sticks together in crumbaloos because she doesn't stir the water. I should make up more words like *crumbaloo*—the exact spot where undercooked strands cling together like sheaves of wheat. The chewy texture is like Twizzlers. Too bad Daddy won't let us eat candy. Anyway, I love rice more than spaghetti. Got to get out of the kitchen before the guilty pot is discovered! I really want to cram in some reading before Steven gets home. Hurry to my bedroom, then the family room at the other end of the house.

What should I read? I wish I still had *Wan-fu: Ten Thousand Happinesses*. I should take it out again from the West Long Branch Public Library. If only I could be rescued like Wan-fu, a crippled Chinese beggar girl; her life had a happy ending. I should read *Sara Crewe* again. Her story is even better than *Wan-fu*. Don't stop and dawdle with Nancy Drew. I'd better grab *Sara Crewe* and rush to the family room.

I wish my life was just a story. Maybe I'm adopted like my cousin Risa or my cousin Stuart, and my real family will come and save me, and I won't have Steven as a brother. Why does Steven have to go everywhere with us? It's so embarrassing when he makes noises at Nunzio's, Howard Johnson's, or Jimmy Lu's Chinese Restaurant. That's not a nice thing to say. I should give thanks because I get to eat out once a week. And Daddy lets me order the ice cream at Howard Johnson's, which has tiny pieces of colored mint candy in it! I wonder if Smitty, the waitress there, likes me. I always tell her how nice she is, so maybe she'll think I'm special. That's right; I should give thanks for what I have. Sara Crewe's father died: left her penniless and she had to move to the attic at Miss Minchin's Select Seminary for Young Ladies. I live in a warm house and can cook myself a pot of rice whenever I want. Sara slaved, and I don't have to do many chores. And even though Sara's life turns around by the end of the book, I don't want Daddy to die!

The family room…not a moment too soon. It's gloomy with dark-wood paneling like a coffin. But shelves are stacked with Daddy's books with intriguing titles like *The Spy Who Came in from the Cold* and *One Flew Over the Cuckoo's Nest*. I've started to read his Ellery Queen mysteries. Daddy's recliner is made of brown Naugahyde, which is as comfortable as real leather. And reading in Daddy's recliner is almost as good as lying in bed reading.

Wouldn't it be groovy to have a job making up product words like Naugahyde and La-Z-Boy? Even more amazing is to be an authoress like Frances Hodgson Burnett who wrote *Sara Crewe*. I love the part about imagination in *Sara Crewe*—which reminds me I haven't started reading yet! Turn right to that part…

Sara's imagination helped her to make everything rather like a story.

"It is a story," Sara would answer. "They are all stories. Everything is a story—everything in this world. You are a story—I am a story—Miss Minchin is a story. You can make a story out of anything."

"Ah. Ehhhh. Ah. Ehhhh. Ah. Ehhhh." Steven is in the house! Can't I just stay here and read? Maybe Steven will go straight to the backyard and walk right by me.

Steven is here! I shield the book in front of my face and try to keep reading. No such luck—Steven is crobbling me! Steven crobbles me! He lurches at me and strokes my bare arm. His fingers tap my skin with a gentle touch like he's tinkling a piano. I get goose bumps.

"Stop, Steven, stop!" I push him. I slap him. I push him. I slap him. I throttle so much that he has to stop crobbling, but he doesn't leave me alone. Then I shout, "I hate you, Steven! I hate you, Steven!" And then, Steven cries. Tears drop from his eyes, soaking his face like the rain when he stands barefoot in the backyard in his pajamas.

It makes no sense to me that Steven is crying. Could it be because I never hit him before? I'm sorry that I did. But I don't want to accept that I've hurt his feelings. It makes no sense to me that he has feelings. I am the one who should be crying, but I'm too angry and confused.

* * *

Why didn't my parents allow my sisters and me to
   lock our doors?
Why were there no family conversations permitting
   the idea
that it was difficult to live
with Steven?

We were expected to accept his behavior because he "doesn't know any better."

Steven could not help himself.
As a child, I could not grasp this.

I do not blame my parents.
I just don't understand why...
We were left on our own a lot as children.
I know they did not mean to do us harm.

Writing this now, I want to go back and make it better.

* * *

I had no words to explain what I was enduring—Steven's lunging tickle-grabbing—so I made up *crobbling*. Just like his blanket yanking, roaming the house, and making noises—I sensed that these behaviors were random and meaningless, but it didn't matter. Steven invaded my space, and I felt powerless.

I have come to accept that Steven didn't know any better. And I understand that his crobbling was innocent. It is possible that crobbling is Steven's way of communicating—to get attention— to express what he cannot put in words.

Debbie and Steven: "reading" together in the living room

Twelve-year-old Debbie: Living room

Cheery sunlight beams through the picture window that faces onto Elmwood Avenue—a big, yellow, smiley face with a Kool-Aid grin. Steven plops onto the couch; he doesn't crobble me! My caution in choosing the armchair, instead of the couch, has won out. I don't jump up to escape, try to continue reading, but I'm distracted.

Steven rattles the pages of a *Good Housekeeping* magazine, click-licking his thumb and fingers against his tongue and flipping the pages so his face and hands are smudged with ink. The pictures glance by him like in a flip book.

"Show me food, Steven; show me food." Steven rattles the pages, touches two fingers to his lips—the only sign language he knows—and points to a photograph of a moist turkey.

Does he realize that Thanksgiving is approaching, when our cousins from New York City will come for dinner? Does Steven enjoy those meals as much as I do? There is plenty of holiday food, but I serve myself everything at once because Steven grabs from plates. I can't risk waiting for seconds. After the meal, I watch *Willie Wonka* with my cousins in the family room before they go back to their apartments. They envy the fact that we live in a house.

At this moment, sitting with Steven in the living room, the food is safe in *Good Housekeeping*. And in the blue hardcover, Nancy Drew lives an exciting but stable life with her father; her boyfriend, Ned Nickerson; and her girlfriends, Bess and George.

If only I had friends like Nancy Drew, who wouldn't laugh at me because I blurted out in class, "What in the world is happening?!" The kids in school don't care about the Vietnam War. They only care about being popular, and making fun of me makes them more popular. I hate those bitches.

If Nancy Drew were real, we would hang out and solve mysteries together. Like the mystery of Steven and what he is thinking. "Slap me five, Steven; slap me five." I salute and Steven slaps his hand against mine.

* * *

By hiding in books, it has taken me years to develop social skills, to make friends and to adapt around people. Although I'm not autistic, I didn't know how to look people in the eye. I still don't do this very well.

Over the years, I've had to teach myself many practical things, like wearing waterproof boots in the snow. I still use bunny ears to tie my shoes. I didn't realize that I had to wash the back of my hair until my thirties.

The Eder family. Winter Break.
Wolfie's delicatessen in Miami Beach

Thirteen-year-old Debbie

The hostess just told Daddy there's a wait for large parties, even though Wolfie's is a multiroom restaurant with many tables and booths. There are eight of us, counting Gramps. The word *party* cracks me up when used to describe my family. So funny, I forgot to laugh. I wish I had an Archie comic book, at least, but I wasn't allowed to bring anything to read. "They're well trained." Daddy once bragged to someone in a restaurant who'd commented that, for so many kids, we're well behaved. That's because Steven stayed put and didn't open his mouth. I hope it doesn't take too long for us to be seated.

I scan the deli to see if anyone is getting up to leave. No such luck. On each table, silver-metal bowls hold glistening pickles, sours, and half-sours. Daddy loves the sour green tomatoes steeped in vinegary brine with pulpy seeds. The food is so good here. I'm going to have a corned beef or a pastrami sandwich on rye, not club bread like Daddy. Maybe I'll have half corned beef/half pastrami and only eat half of it. I have to watch what I eat because I just lost a lot of weight, and pastrami and corned beef are fattening. Mommy and Liz are always trying to get Daddy to stay on a diet. For Chanukah, we gave him a sort of Hummel plastic statue, that I named Chubble, with a pudgy endearing Charlie Brown face. Plump Chubble is seated on a plaque step on which the phrase is carved "I'm a Weight Watcher. Please don't feed me." Chubble reminds me of Fred Flintstone, who is also like Daddy. Daddy will probably compromise tonight by ordering health salad instead of cole slaw. And diet Dr. Brown's Celray tonic soda. Steven is big and husky and not at all cute like

Chubble. It's a good thing that there's a lock on our refrigerator, so he can't eat everything up.

More people push through the door and crowd against my family.

"Ah de chuck a lay.

Ah de chuck a lay.

Leh coco lie.

Leh coco lie.

Leh coco lie."

Steven pulls away from Daddy and starts to run into the restaurant. Daddy takes after him.

"Ah. Ehhhh.

Ah. Ehhhh.

Ah. Ehhhh."

"Can't you restrain him??!" a woman exclaims. She has a look on her face like Steven is some kind of animal. "He has no choice!" I shout.

* * *

This is not a story with a happy ending.

Neither is it a sad story.

I left 19 Elmwood Avenue after high school, graduated from an Ivy League university, and achieved a Master's degree in creative writing. I've held good jobs. Now middle-aged, I pass for an attractive, sometimes poised, slender woman with long hair in a ponytail who wears basic black with funky accessories— appropriate for New York City where I live in an apartment with my significant other. It is our home.

My brother Steven left 19 Elmwood Avenue around the same time I did. He lives in a supervised group home with other autistic men and spends his days at a sheltered workshop. I can't imagine him doing any work; he still can't wash his hair. My mother takes him out on Sundays; my father passed away several years ago.

* * *

I have fought with Steven to find my voice.
But that doesn't change Steven.
I do love my brother.
I haven't seen him in years.
I call him on his birthday,
and he holds the phone to his ear,
but he never says a word.

We Were Beautiful, Once

9

My Autistic-
American Family

Maureen McDonnell

Another young family lived behind us in a suburban house facing the main street. When we were little and my dad worried less about his back, our fathers would hoist up one child, then another, for each family to admire. When we are a bit older, we are passed over the sagging fence. This handing over, always executed under careful eyes, became in my memory a vibrant flinging of children, air and sunlight between the body and fence as we are hurled to safety and a set of waiting arms.

A few years ago, the mothers and daughters went out to dinner. Sue hauls out one of my favorite stories about her now-dead Irish setter who tore into our trash cans thirty years ago and, through his destruction, introduced our families. But Sue stops midway and fixes her gaze on her daughter.

"You know, I kept telling Lou when you were kids, when he began complaining. I said to look at their family. Look at Dianne and Rich. They have three beautiful children." She looks at me to aim this story home. "But we have healthy children. Don't you dare complain about anything in our house."

My mother begins to discuss the shortcake. I can't tell from her face if she had ever heard Sue say this before. But I think gratefully of Sue's offering all the way home. We were beautiful, at least.

* * *

I have spent my life passing, trying to prove that genetics are a fluke, that my parents aren't incapable of raising children, that my life is neatly my own. My stubbornness helped me fulfill the trappings of the successful child. When I finished graduate school, my brother Dave announced the news to everyone he met. I have knowingly placed myself in a profession where intellect and alertness are immeasurably important goods. I like knowing that the ability to explain a subordinate clause helps pay my bills. Still, I resist believing that there is any virtue in having your relationship with words or ideas result in having dozens of students, a sofa, a life. For nearly everyone who knows my family, I am only, ever, my brothers' sister.

With few kids our age on our block, my brothers, Dave and Mark, were forced to play house, GI Joe, and school with me, the youngest of the trio. I wore their hand-me-downs, tried to imitate their outdoor peeing techniques, and returned the bite marks they sometimes left on my arms. These experiences, along with a handful of orange-tinted photos from the 1970s, are our argument for having had a happy childhood. We like each other as adults. We hold down jobs, have relationships that matter to us, share proud parents. Dave, now in his late thirties, is our family's publicist, remembering everyone he meets and their birthdates. Dave has my dad's pale skin and blue eyes, some gray hair, and an expression of eager expectation. Mark has a good jump shot. He tans like my mother, wears his hair as short as possible, and insists on black tee-shirts, loose collars, and complete meals. We all dwarf our parents and share sturdy, muscular shoulders.

However, for many people my brothers' autism is the only aspect of their personalities worth mentioning. Their diagnosis suggests that they are oblivious to the people around them, that they live in a whirl of motion and silence, that we can never know them as people instead of cases.

Well.

I know that Dave tries to schedule dinners with me months before my visits home, coercing me to visit his workplace so that I can see him wearing his etched nametag and stocking shelves. Mark can call out for me, "Moowhee," the inflection right if the pronunciation wrong, and my body twists toward him almost before I hear the vibrations of his voice. I find satisfaction in the way his torso rocks forward on the second syllable, the grin there at that word, as if the sound of my name is enough to penetrate whatever science condemns him into, as though that word is enough to bring him joy.

Despite the public's rising interest in autistic children, my adult brothers remain vulnerable and, largely, ignored. We are a relatively lucky family. We love and like each other. Dave and Mark have the ability to speak, to recognize and interact with us, and (in Mark's case) to make a pretty good stir-fry. Still, notions of the cold "refrigerator" parent persisted until the mid-1980s, too late for us to have received something like compassion in the waiting rooms we occupied throughout my childhood. By the time David, the oldest of us, was three, his hyperactivity had labeled him as a "problem," Mark's talking had stopped as suddenly as it had begun, and my upcoming entrance into the family became evident. Our family became complete on the doubled diagnosis of autism and the arrival of me, the normal child.

It is difficult for the so-called normal child to grow up in a house where watching Popeye cartoons at a certain time is of paramount importance or to learn that errands outside can result in stares, gawking, threats, or calls to Children's Protective Services. As a kid, I wanted to backtalk the adults who glared at my brothers in public as though they were less than human. It's difficult to witness considerable gaffes when disabilities are discussed (the illiteracy on this matter by well-read people continues to surprise me), sparking my long-standing, finely honed need to shield my brothers. Many parents' memoirs of their autistic children tend to glide over disruption, expense, and chaos to make their families more presentable to outsiders. The voices of siblings like me are both more ambivalent and absent. When reports make us "normal" siblings the subjects of the scientific gaze, I bristle—and not just because I resent being defined as a casualty of my brothers' disabilities, whether the "normal" siblings are cast as damaged or nurturing. The premise makes sense: I am the default, the norm; I am, in theory, the representative of what didn't go wrong. I know the power and privileges that come from being seen as normal. I live in a world filled with language, keenly aware that language is painful terrain for the people I love most. Yet I can't find in the data or in my own life easy ways to explain why my brothers haunt and comfort me or the childhood that we still share. Uneasily, then, I remain willful enough to imagine that my perspective on who I am and who my brothers are might count.

I can say that my three-year-old self felt unease and fear, never pride, when I began to run, count, learn faster than my big brothers (my own intelligence, confirmed on the many tests that my worried parents insisted on, highlighted my brothers' deficiencies). I don't like remembering that I became the third parent in my family by the time I was twelve. I felt abandoned in my thirties when family friends (who had pledged to be a resource for my aging parents) moved without mentioning their promise. I hated asking my best friend to be my logistical and legal back-up. She didn't blink before saying yes. I am the one ashamed to have asked such a big favor for my parents' children. My parents talk with relief about her commitment and mine, if not about their children's past. My brothers' disability means that my parents have no nostalgia about our childhood. We, as children, gave them so little they wanted to remember.

Their disability hurt me. It changed me. I hurt for them, often. And yet, we were a family that ate dinner together every night, who destroyed Tonka trunks, who were read to by my father, and were calmed at the sound of my mother's singing. And Dave and Mark taught me about my flaws and my worth. I know that I love well and can (in their case) love fiercely. In my brothers' faces, in the rocking of their bodies, my childhood is preserved: not a static relic of the past but a fluid, shifting testament to their—to our—endurance. And I have an advantage in knowing that the things that have harmed my family are, for the most part, natural disasters beyond our control.

* * *

When I am three or four, before Mark leaves us in 1980, he kicks a hole in his bedroom door. He kicks the plaster with his bare feet, breaking nothing inside his body. Mark moves back and forth from his room to the carpeted hallway, grinning his missing-teeth smile. I line up behind him, on all fours, and pummel my own way through. The game finally ends when we are found by our parents, herding ourselves through the plaster dust and jagged edges.

A picture of me in first grade that year shows the Strawberry Shortcake-print dress my mother made. I wear the medical-identification bracelet that I asked for, one "just like" my brothers'. The outside curves of their bracelets list their names, our address, phone number, and state; the wrist side includes the words "mental retardation/autism." (Autism wasn't well known enough at the time to be understandable to most medical personnel.) The inside of my bracelet has an etching of a saint and asks its reader to, "in case of emergency, please call a priest." Slung over my shoulder is the book bag sewn by my mother, complete with rick-rack on the edges and my name in glitter iron-transfer letters. I stand by the front door of our house, my eyes fixed not on the camera but down at the flowerpot at my right.

Mark left our house a few months earlier. His frustration at not being able to speak showed itself in the new holes in our walls, in the bruises he gave himself, in my downward shifted glance. His new home in Sacramento believed in vitamins, in sign language, in behavior modification, in exercise, and in regular visits. For twelve years, my mother and I made the six-hour trek to Sacramento and back to pick up and return Mark twice each month.

As an adult, I learned that the decision to "place" Mark tore up my father who approached our childhood hoping to resolve the pain of his. He saw Mark's placement as abandonment—despite the glossy brochure, despite the obvious good the home's program did for Mark. My mother, juggling three demanding children and a withdrawn husband, saw the program as a refuge and as a chance to satisfy the needs of at least one person in the family. In the hope of a cure, my parents tried carob chips, group homes, stuffed animals, play therapy, family therapy, and prayer. I tried being good enough to redeem us all. Later on, I would see the group home as the only way Mark could have been brought back to us, saved from the fate of silence and seclusion that would certainly have awaited him had he been born ten years earlier.

My mom knew something was wrong with Dave when Mark was born, knew that Mark was having trouble by the time I came along. At first, according to the doctors in the 1970s, she was an overprotective, smothering mother. These normal developmental delays were, they said, nothing that would matter in a few months. If she would just relax and stop hovering, they would be fine. She tried to believe their directive. She must have been relieved when Mark, finally, began to talk. At age two, just as suddenly, he stopped. When he was hungry, she would begin pointing at the top shelf of the cupboards, moving her index finger down one shelf at a time. When he finally nodded, she would move her finger along (left to right, since that's how children learn to read, and she wanted him to be ready) as she named each item until he nodded. Usually, they were both in tears by the time her finger rested on whatever he wanted.

She brought this news to the doctor's, insisting that he and Dave both be retested and not knowing (despite her nursing background) which tests to ask for. She sat in the office, trying to prevent Mark from pushing the emergency button that summoned security, holding on to Dave with the other hand, a foot, whatever was available. This time, the doctor accused her of being a cold, unfeeling mother. If she could only find it in herself to love her children a little bit more, perhaps these oddities would clear up. Had the various doctors agreed on how she was ruining her children, perhaps she would have believed them. As it was, she began fostering her own obstinacy, her skepticism of doctors, and faith in her children's resilience—choices that undoubtedly protected all three of us and my father at different moments. But as she protected her children from the voices outside our home, her own attitude toward her profession began to falter.

She began to tutor me in the differences between my family and others, to speak out against the guilt she was supposed to feel: "Maureen, there are parents who do horrible, unspeakable things to their children. But those kids still grow up."

Now an adult, I take my mother's message to mean that these anonymous abused children eventually become adults who can read novels, slug down a Guinness, carry a passport. They could escape whatever terrors their families had visited on them. As I grew up, I saw how my status as the "little sister" drew sighs from the other mothers of "special children" (as they were known in the 1980s) who appeared in different degrees of doggedly cheerful and bone tired. They turned from me and my Nancy Drew books to watch one brother or another ricochet off gym walls. They imagined aloud that we normal kids could escape and have lives of our own. They carefully prepared us, too, to take care of children who were not ours: in the short term, in the decades ahead. We knew better than to ask how we were to live those contradictions.

What was never spoken—and was always present—is the recognition that I, who suffered no unspeakable things, who is decisively healthy, would grow up. I had to grow up, and not think too much about how I want to ask my brothers' blessing as I write or their forgiveness for loving this life that I have. I had to grow up, or my parents might be seen as failures. I had to grow up because these men, my brothers, can't.

* * *

133

One evening when I am six, I sob in the bed I inherited from Grandpa Mac. I can't be certain why Mark isn't in the house. I like its quiet. No one sneaks into my room to play my Hungry Hippos game, waking me up with laughter and the smack of marbles against plastic mechanical mouths. I'm not certain why we make the trek to the large ranch house where Mark now lives. My hands know words now and can say "I want," "I feel" by moving through space in particular ways. I can even spell my name by focusing on my fingers. What I don't know is what I might be risking with each tantrum, whether at some point I would push my parents too far and earn my own exile from the family.

My mother hears my crying and sits on my bed. I still hate this memory. I say something about how much fun Mark can be, that I want him living in his room and not with strangers. That I can share better, behave better. I know, for certain, that I ask if she and Daddy are thinking of sending me away, too. At this point, my mother's face crumbles, worse than when my grandpa Mac died.

"Missy, I miss him too. He's my baby." I want to correct her—I, the youngest, am her baby, but I am lost in the shock of making my mother cry. She tells me that I am staying here, that this is my home, that she is my mother. I thought all those things were true for Mark, whose room is empty. I decide to believe there aren't plans for me to leave, at least not yet. She holds onto me, both our faces sticky. The next morning I try to pretend that nothing had happened. But my eyes keep slipping down from my mother's all-seeing glance to look at the latest smudge on my shoes. I can't manage to look up.

* * *

When I am ten, there is a new blood test out. With two autistic children, both boys, and a younger daughter who tested as gifted, my family sometimes catches a researcher's eye. These researchers think that perhaps Fragile X syndrome is related to autism.

With a blood draw that will be (my parents promise) quick, the researchers could at least rule Fragile X out.

My mother tells me in the car that my brothers will have other tests as well. I'm spared most of them, thanks to being female and not having hit puberty yet. My brothers each need to have their testes measured, since small testicles can signal certain disorders. I have seen them naked for years, because standing naked in the hallway reminds my parents that shower time is shower time. But the logistics of measuring are beyond me. My mom notices my quietness and begins to compare the measuring instruments to plastic Easter eggs. Thanks to car rides like this, I know more about sex than anyone in my class. I begin to hide in my room at shower time, unwilling that anyone might see more of my brothers than they should.

The researcher sits with us weeks later at our kitchen table, the only time I remember a scientist in our house. I am given another crash course in genetics, part of the curriculum for kids like me who know surprising amounts about the moments of development that can veer horribly off track. Children like me know that we are always, always, meant to see ourselves as the lucky ones. This time, my parents and I are shown the separate case files. No break in the chromosome. No Fragile X. Now my brothers are, for once, the lucky ones. And I am told to be pleased as well because, by the time I'm old enough (the researcher tells me), there will be better tests so that my children will be safe.

He is a scientist and an adult. But I am a smart fourth-grader. I've done fractions at school. I still think my odds are bad. Less than a C minus. I haven't had my first monthly period, and already I think that I will never marry, but I will have a daughter. I began to think of her name. I do my best to never, ever, let myself imagine a son.

* * *

When I am about eleven years old, we begin looking into group homes for David. Adolescence is especially cruel on autistic boys, as its standard surge of hormones is wreaked upon minds that are frequently not capable of dealing with the assault. (My own body wasn't ready for the literal assaults of Dave, which placed me in a hospital emergency room twice before he moved to his group home in the late 1980s.) Dave, Mom, and I visit an open house where kids are eating deviled eggs, potato chips, and Oreo cookies. I sit by my mother's side for the first hour, apart from the swinging arms and loud humming that lash out here.

A woman I knew begins talking about a kid that had been in Dave's class only a few years ago. I like his crooked smile and his mellowness. As the conversation continues, I learn that he entered the state institution, Agnews, last June and had been drugged up so badly that he was no longer capable of talking. A staff member then forced him to lie down and began to jump on his stomach. The worker was fired, but the institution can't legally warn anyone else of the abuse. This worker could get hired again and again to care for mentally disabled or mentally ill patients. And this faceless man, the mothers conclude, is why group homes are a good idea.

I sit beside my mother on the car ride home. Mom drives us past Agnew's, the adobe building and vast lawns giving it the air of a college campus instead of an institution. I remind her that Dave and Mark are not crazy, that this is where crazy people go. She asks me if I remember a kid in Dave's childhood-adapted recreation program. She tells me, "He's a runner, you know. He likes to run away. And once he got himself completely lost on a day that his grandma was visiting. His mom was about to call the police before her own mother asked, 'Is it such a loss if he doesn't come back?' She still called the police, though."

I try to imagine this exchange as I stare at the institution. Your own family may turn on you. You, lost, could be a blessing to them.

* * *

136

When I am sixteen, I visit my great aunt Maddie in her Midwestern home that she and her deceased husband built together. The land had become the most valuable thing she owned, as strip malls had began, kudzu-like, to engulf the territory. We go to a teen movie that she chooses. My great aunts generally fawn over David with a generosity that I appreciate more than they know. Mark, who becomes anxious in strange places and in crowds, hasn't visited my grandparents in years. The visit would almost certainly spark shrieking and a round of Mark's wall- or Mark-punching; neither our nerves nor my grandparents' home are up for that.

Maddie and I talk about my brother David: his handsomeness, his cheerfulness, his willingness to stampede toward strangers and offer his hand wrong side up. I am used to sentimental platitudes about my brothers. I am "stronger" for knowing these men that will never be men. We are blessed. My parents have suffered so. My mother is a saint. But Aunt Maddie leans to her left, so that her dyed hair just rasps against my ear. "Really, your brother, it's such a waste."

I can say nothing throughout the rest of the movie. I would have rather she slapped me. Family stories get us through the rest of the visit. My grandfather heaves himself into the house to pick me up. I follow him into the Chevy and quiver all the way back to the farm.

I announce to my grandmother that I am never visiting Aunt Maddie again. The comment seemed less hurtful in the stoicism of my grandmother's kitchen. I try my protest aloud: "David is not a waste. He's not. He's as good as anyone else." Grandma tries to convince me of Maddie's good intentions. I've watched Grandma shove dessert bars and extra helpings onto Dave's plate each meal, her taciturn way of offering love. But I can tell from her pursed lips that she too has said things like this. If not in my hearing.

* * *

137

In the state of California, all parents of disabled adults need to take (often expensive) legal action if they wish to continue their parenting. My parents decided to file for conservatorship of their sons; otherwise, we were warned, Dave and Mark could announce that they were leaving their treatment programs and nothing could be done. Each of my brothers' rights was carefully listed and catalogued: the right to phone conversations, to practice their religion, to sexual activities. My parents check off each one. My mom took care of registering them for military service, then filled out the paperwork explaining why the armed forces would want to reject them.

Shortly after Dave turned eighteen, I'd deliberate over my prom dress, finally begin driver's education, and enter a second year of calculus before college. I take a day off from school to visit the lawyer with my parents and make conservatorship official. I wear a flowered dress. I sign where I am told. I say that I, when I am able, will take care of my brothers after our parents die. This afternoon is one of the proudest in my life, the commitment the largest I have ever made. This moment, this signing of my name, is the closest I ever got to being a teenage mother.

During the early 1990s, my mom lectures me after night shifts in the obstetrics ward. On a standard morning, I would spoon yogurt into my mouth, while she talked of girls my age and their too-narrow pelvises. She says to me what she cannot say to them: "We did everything right. I nursed all you kids. No alcohol, I've never smoked, and I even held off on cold syrup. And these people, these *children*, they see a smiling baby has its fingers and think everything's fine. But it's not. You kids looked fine, too. I want to shake them, tell them to wait a few years. Tell them to wait and see how healthy that kid is then."

Even then, I envied those teenage mothers: they chose their dependents. I'll inherit four of them: both brothers, both parents. The girls in the hospital don't share the sense of doom that I sometimes feel.

* * *

drive the point home. But I stay there, unwilling for the speaker to relax, determined to make them all uncomfortable, so that my presence might make my brothers visible. The little boy is told he shouldn't say that, not that. I manage to hold on to my spot on the couch for a few more minutes. I then leave for the humming kitchen where my mother sits to help her sort through the many ways in which she can bury her gentle, loving dad.

* * *

Dave is obsessed with Mass; the autistic person's passion for ritual happens to find an affinity in our family's religion. He can't always say the words as quickly as the congregation, but he knows the rhythms exactly and sings along to the murmurs around us. Long prayers are our cue to grasp onto an arm and keep him in the aisle before he rushes toward a friend. When I was in second grade, my mother revamped her wedding veil for my first communion. David got a new plaid shirt and a tie (a suit wouldn't have accommodated his swaying). Together, we padded up the center aisle to present the gifts. I tried to overlook the whispers, the sympathetic smiles, the flash bulbs that our walk inspired. I still try to cultivate Dave's particular gift of being able to ignore those things around me that don't suit me.

My dad took an adult Dave to reconciliation during a pre-Easter home visit. The church has begun to have communal penance services, with each parishioner heading up and offering his top few sins. Think of fast-food drive-ins, and you have the idea. But we've never said the word *sin* to Dave. His religious-education classes (again, the "special" class) stopped before the sinning began, before pardoning was needed. On this evening, Dave heads up before Dad. Reconciliation is utterly new territory. Dave pauses before the priest, obviously unable to remember the time since his last confession. Instead, he rocks back and forth and stops to announce, "I love Jesus." The priest glances at this normal-looking young man in perpetual motion, then at my stooped father. He doesn't ask questions, just places his hand on

Dave's forehead to begin blessing him. It's not a cute story to me, not something precious. It signals that he got something *right*. That finally someone in our family has slipped past guilt and penance and can distil catechism into four syllables.

* * *

I left California when I was twenty-one. When I return, one of my favorite spaces is behind the driver's wheel with one of my brothers beside me. Mark is the calmer passenger. We coach each other through his morning rituals, taking turns asking, "And then what?" We talk about food, *Sesame Street, Mr. Rogers' Neighborhood.* Anything I say is okay with him, but I keep trying to get his perfect day right. We stop for ice cream. We drive nowhere. We trade sentences back and forth. He helps me remember how good it feels to sit next to a person that you love, a good man who wants nothing more than to grin at you and say yes, yes, over and over again.

One evening Dave and I headed on to the Alameda Expressway, lurching as I shift my car up into fifth gear. His sense of direction is better than mine, so he usually navigates. The Clash comes on. Dave begins to laugh and flick his fingertips together. His rocking begins to match the beat of the song. And he begins, incredibly, to sing, to "rock the cas-bah." It takes me a split second, but then my wrist flicks up the volume, and the two of us are screaming along, rocking away, rocking out, both bodies a blur of volume and giddiness. I roll down the window, spilling our music into the whipping sound of traffic.

* * *

I want to end this by giving you that open road and the buzz of connection. I finish writing this on an early morning. My feet are bare and my elbows ache. I've spent my lifetime trying to say goodbye to possibilities. There is no set way to grieve for the men my brothers might have been, for how my parents might

144

have aged without their disabled sons and a defiant daughter, or for me. Alone I'm left to ask what we might mean to each other: Mark's rituals and physical grace; Dave's greetings of total strangers, in which he never falters or imagines rejections. And there I am, witness to it all, cradling warm coffee mugs, soaking in comfort from the small spaces that it can be found. I lean back to say this: our love is part of the world I live in. I see us all, see our beauty, this grace. I see it still.

Holding On 10

Lindsey Fisch

Some memories, resisting our efforts to hold them, slip away with time. Experiences that were not emotionally evocative do not earn a "spot" in our precious memory banks. Even mundane activities, however, may be recalled vaguely if they occurred routinely. This is how I think of Sundays during my teenage years. I remember these days as a time to "catch up" with all those necessary tasks that must be completed before Monday morning. I remember towering laundry piles, procrastinated homework, and expensive grocery-store runs. One memory of a Sunday in October 2003, however, stands out as anything but mundane and one that will forever stay with me.

Everything seemed to be running as planned. My dad had taken my brother Daniel to hockey practice, and they were expected home in an hour. I sat on the couch in the family room, television on for background noise, methodically plugging away at my precalculus homework. My mom and my brother Adam worked together to try and conquer the week's dirty laundry. She stayed in the laundry room, while Adam took his position upstairs in my parents' bedroom. After stripping the beds of their bedsheets, he would throw the dirty sheets down the clothes chute. Adam took great pleasure in his job, loving the consistency of routine and watching the sheets slide down. His autism in this regard was an advantage. Adam would carefully place the corner of the sheet into the clothes chute and slowly release it, apparently enjoying the slight "whoosh" of the sheet as he let go. My mom would praise him from the laundry room: "Thank you, sweetie. Good job!" Echoing up through the fifteen-foot-long metal chute, these words of praise always made Adam smile. Like any eight-year-old child, he thrived on verbal praise. Typically, on completing his duties, Adam would march down the stairs like a trained soldier. Although he was tiny for his age at forty-eight pounds, his feet hit each step with the force of a 150-pound man. On this day, however, the pounding footsteps did not resound through the house. Its absence probably registered somewhere in the back of our minds, but we did not recognize its portent.

As my mom entered the family room, arms full of lavender-scented laundry, she asked if I could watch Adam while she ran to the grocery store. I agreed and returned to my homework, hoping to finish before I would be on duty to watch Adam. With the nine-year age gap between the two of us, I had grown accustomed to being a handy and reliable babysitter, one my parents could almost always count on to be there and understand my brother. My mom proceeded upstairs with the laundry. As she climbed the stairs, I heard her calling, "A-dam!" Silence. Climbing a few more steps, "Adam, where are you?" Still nothing. Although basically nonverbal, Adam always responded to his name with some sort of vocalization or would appear to see what was wanted.

Turning to my homework, I blocked out my mom's calls. Over the years, my capacity for selective attention had been perfected, courtesy of Adam's video rituals. Like many children with autism, Adam loved to listen repeatedly to select parts of his favorite videos. Overtaken by his compulsion, he would continually rewind a video to the exact same scene. I cannot even begin to count the number of times I have heard special parts of *Barney*, *Winnie the Pooh*, and *Richard Scarry* videos. Song lyrics have been imprinted in my mind; I am able to recite them as if I were a child obsessed with the videos myself. I hear the running soundtrack of busy people working hard all over town and the persistent echo of Pooh Bear's love of honey, the yum, yum, yums, and his wish for something sweet. Living in a home where Disney sing-along songs are part of everyday language, I had learned to tune out practically all external noise in order to focus on my work. My excellent selective attention, however, did not screen out my mother's strident call from upstairs: "*Lindsey! Call 9-1-1!*"

Hearing the numbers 9-1-1 prompted both urgency and a memory. I first learned that these numbers signified a state of emergency when I was five-years-old. My mom's admonition still called out in my mind: "Only dial 9-1-1 for *real* emergencies, never pranks or jokes." Always curious to test boundaries, when I was around six, I dialed 9-1-1 because my other brother, Daniel, who was four at the time, had double-dog-dared me to call. "You're such a scaredy cat," he taunted, waving the phone in my face. Wanting to prove I was fearless about calling the forbidden number, I ignored the tightening feeling in my stomach and quickly dialed the phone. The operator responded to my call after one ring: "9-1-1, emergency." Shocked at what I had done, I promptly hung up. Daniel was impressed, his brown curls bouncing up and down as he tugged on my arm. "What'd they say?" He would never be able to call me a scaredy cat again, I thought. Then the phone rang. My dad answered. "I am so sorry. There is no emergency here." He turned slowly and looked directly at me—the look on his face was one of immense disappointment. I gave up the idea of denying my actions and accepted my grounding without argument, vowing to call 9-1-1 only in the event of a true emergency. Eleven emergency-free years had passed. For a moment, however, I felt paralyzed, held by a distant memory. Find the phone, Lindsey. Find it *now*.

My heart raced as I jumped up from the couch. Where is the phone? Why do we have portable phones? Why the heck do people never put the phone back where it belongs? Panicked, I raced up the stairs, taking two at a time, to grab the phone in my parents' bedroom. Turning into the bedroom, I came to a sudden halt. Lodged up to his armpits in the clothes chute, arms and head at an awkward angle, Adam whimpered, his face ghostly white and eyes glass-like. My mom knelt, trying to pull him gently from the laundry chute, her face just as white as his. She knew Adam now had adrenocortical insufficiency in addition to his autism and epilepsy. His body was unable to release life-saving cortisol in response to stress.

Was this really happening? How did he get in there? How did he fit? It reminded me of a scene from one of our Winnie the Pooh videos, a scene Adam had played repeatedly showing Pooh lodged in Rabbit's front door and all his friends from Pooh Corner trying to pull him out. Was Adam trying to be like Pooh? I recalled Adam reenacting the scene with a kitchen chair. Often contorting his body underneath the chair rungs, he satisfied his need for tactile stimulation and his imitation of Pooh being stuck. My brother and I were always amazed he could even fit underneath the chair. Indeed, emerging from the contortionist position, Adam's triumphant smile would shout, "I told you so!" But maybe he was not trying to be Pooh. He might have envisioned the chute as a slide like his favorite part of the playground. Who could know? As I grabbed the phone and dialed 9-1-1, my hands trembled. I whispered soft prayers to myself, hoping that I would be able to get help for my brother. The operator picked up immediately, saying the same words I heard during my prank call when I was six: "9-1-1, emergency."

I stuttered at first but forced myself to remain calm and speak coherently. "My brother is stuck in the laundry chute. He's autistic, and we can't get him out. Please help." The operator paused briefly, typing the information and then asked with a sense of puzzlement in her voice, "He's where?" In tears, I anxiously replied, "He's stuck in the laundry chute, and we can't pull him out. You have to help!" As I looked at Adam, I could hear my mom trying to suppress the trembling in her voice in an effort to calm him: "Hang in there, sweetie. You hold on." Still kneeling in pain on her bad knee, she took his small, pale hands between her own. She could feel the cool sweat of his skin rub on her palms. Giving him "love squeezes" and forcing her head up high to prevent tears from rolling down her face, she continued to reassure him softly: "Everything will be okay. We'll get you out, baby." My mom, a physician who had been trained to remain calm in emergency situations, struggled to maintain her composure.

Only a few months earlier, Adam had gone into shock after vomiting. I had been babysitting Adam when I noticed him grow incredibly pale and lethargic almost instantaneously. Looking as if he were about to heave all over the living-room carpet, I quickly picked him up and ran to the bathroom. I propped him over the toilet; he nearly collapsed. "Adam! Baby!" I called, shaking him slightly to check his alertness. His body was floppy, and a cool sweat had started to form on his forehead. I reached for the cell phone in my jean pocket to call my mom. The call went straight to her voicemail. I called her beeper, typing in as the call-back number, "9-1-1." Wrapping a towel around Adam to warm him, I softly spoke to him: "Mommy's almost here, sweetie." My heart raced and my muscles tightened as I stared at my brother who lay helpless across my lap. I watched Adam's chest rise and fall, decelerating with each breath. My right forearm grew numb as I continued to support the weight of his upper body. Taking my free hand, I ran my fingers gently through his chestnut-brown hair, remembering how my mom would comfort me when I had the flu. Small beads of sticky sweat gathered on my fingers. His body felt so cold. I held Adam closer, hearing his breathing grow increasingly shallow. A sense of inadequacy came over me. A child almost always calls out for "Mommy" when ill. I could only think how much Adam wanted to be comforted by our mother's loving touch. I was thankful when my mom rushed through the door about a minute later. "*Mom, help!*" I screamed. She ran into the bathroom and looked down at Adam's chalky, ragdoll form. Silently, she scooped him up, and we raced to the emergency room, both of us in unspoken pain, silent tears sliding down our cheeks, praying that we would be in time.

Adam was seen immediately by doctors in the emergency room, and we quickly learned that his body temperature was dangerously low and his oxygen levels had significantly dropped. After spending nearly four hours in the emergency room, Adam responded well to intravenous fluids and steroids, but the doctors admitted him to the pediatric intensive-care unit for the night to continue observation. Shortly thereafter, testing confirmed that Adam had acquired adrenocortical insufficiency. On the refrigerator in the kitchen, we posted a laminated letter from the pediatric endocrinologist providing instructions to any emergency-room physician should acute emergency arise in the future. The words from the letter flashed before my eyes. "Adam has secondary adrenocortical insufficiency. He requires 1mg/kg body weight of intravenous steroids in settings of stress such as trauma, vomiting, or fever." With no steroids available, Adam grew weaker and paler each second. I grew impatient with the operator, "You have to hurry! He's going into shock!" The operator assured me that police and fire teams were responding to the scene. Being asked persistently more and more questions, I tried to remain calm to answer queries about Adam's condition. My mom relayed information to me: "Faint pulse, clammy." Please help him, I prayed. God, please do not let him die here.

When the doorbell finally rang, I raced downstairs to fling open the door. A policeman in his late fifties stood in front of me. He entered the house and ran upstairs behind me, the floorboards vibrating violently. On seeing Adam, he radioed in an update to the rescue workers en route. He then tried to help my mom pull Adam loose. The siren from the fire truck could now be heard. It blipped off in front of the house. Soon the booted feet of three firemen pounded up the stairs. One of them carried a small emergency kit. As they reached the top of the stairs, they noticed my brother's bedroom, complete with fire engine quilt and pictures of fire trucks on the wall. One of them called out, "Hey! The kid likes fire trucks!" "In *here*," my mother called. The firemen, too, tried to pull Adam out of the laundry chute. All the physical strength and no one could pull that forty-eight-pound child out of his trap. Then my mother called out: "Olive oil! Lindsey, we need the olive oil!"

I pounded down the stairs, grabbed a big bottle of Kirkland's extra-virgin olive oil from the kitchen, and tore back upstairs. My mom took the oil and poured it wherever there was a miniscule opening between Adam and his trap. It slopped on the floor as she shook the container, but a good amount found its way into the clothes chute. Trying to fit her hand into the chute to spread the oil over my brother's small body, she experienced some difficulty. "Mom, let me try. My hand's smaller," I said. Like an acrobat, I contorted my own body at awkward angles, stretching my arm as far down the laundry chute as I could to reach all the nonlubricated spots. With nearly half the bottle of olive oil gone, I pulled my arm out of the laundry chute. Adam was still clammy and lethargic, only rarely whimpering now. Two firemen took him by the arms. Crouched under the chute, my mom squeezed her hands under his armpits and pushed forward slightly to protect his back from scraping against the metal and wooden edge of the chute. "On a count of three, pull!" Adam moved slightly, and my mom could now fit her two hands under his armpits. They pulled again, and Adam started to slide, inch by inch, out of the clothes chute. The firemen laid him on the floor and checked his vital signs, while my mother covered him with a blanket and rubbed him vigorously. Warmer, Adam looked at my mom and then gazed at all the strange faces around the room as she carried him into the bathroom to run a warm bath.

Adam responded well to the bath and oral steroids. The policeman and one of the firemen followed my mom into the bathroom to take down a report of the incident. It now became somewhat humorous. How many times will you need to rescue someone stuck in a laundry chute? Adam splashed around in the bathtub, oblivious to the recent terror, scooping and pouring bathwater with a pitcher. Grinning, one of the firemen entered with a plastic fireman's hat. My mom pulled Adam out of the tub, wrapping him in a towel. The fireman presented Adam with the gift, saying, "I saw your quilt had fire trucks all over them." He then opened the blinds of the bathroom window; Adam looked outside. Parked in front of our house, the beautiful, red fire truck shone in the sun, its lights still flashing. Adam smiled and put the hat on. As the fireman and policeman left, my mom expressed her immense gratitude for their help and quick response. As she shut the door behind them, however, she said in a joking tone, "That fireman just reinforced Adam's behavior! I hope the little guy has been out of the chute long enough not to connect the two events!"

My dad and brother came home about ten minutes later. Adam appeared as though nothing had happened to him. Just a typical Sunday with plenty of laundry to do! Now warm, dry, and treated with steroids, Adam bounced up and down on his favorite yellow ball, trying to keep his new fireman's hat atop his head. Quite happy, he appeared to have already "bounced back" from the incident. I, on the other hand, had not yet recovered from the trauma. I would never look at things the same way again. It is only now, over five years later, that I can relive the memory and hold on to the lessons I learned from it without reliving the anxiety of the actual event.

Similar to witnessing Adam's shock episode a few months earlier, seeing Adam trapped in the laundry chute was like reality seizing me, shaking me, even slapping me in the face. Trapped in a tight space, literally hanging on for his life, his seeming reenactment of Pooh or attempt to slide down a big slide had failed. A sense of terror and angst came over me. Everything seemed beyond my control. All I could do was imagine how Adam must have felt. Unable to communicate his pain and fear, he hung motionless, innocent of the real danger that he could lose his life. His handsome, smiling face and beautiful eyes were nearly vacant, void of an animating sparkle and shine. Adam was autistic, not the happy, engaging, talking toddler he had been before he regressed. We all loved him anyway—if possible, even more since his regression. He was an innocent, vulnerable, gentle, different, special, achingly adorable baby brother who, in many ways, would likely remain a "baby" to my family all his life.

Looking back, there were moments during the episode when I stared at his lethargic, pale body and tried to revitalize him through memory. I recalled the two of us sliding down slides, roller-blading, taking biweekly trips to the library to pick out his favorite videos. I imagined Adam carrying out his nightly routine, giving everyone a soft goodnight kiss on the cheek, albeit prompted. I could hear him slowly and laboriously recite a saying my mom had said to all her children since we were very young: "I luf you to pie-ces. I'll al-ways luf you to pie-ces, and don't you ef-fer for-get it." This incident distilled for me life's fragility. A stupid clothes chute was going to seize my brother from me—someone I loved beyond description—abilities, disabilities, and all.

When I headed off to college, the transition was somewhat difficult at first. Living on my own, not having class every day, and developing a new social network, I simultaneously felt excited and anxious. I would make frequent phone calls home to detail the study-abroad sites I was considering and report how things were going. I was able to communicate my experiences to my parents and Daniel, but finding a way to maintain a relationship with Adam was difficult. How could I bridge the physical distance between us when he was predominantly nonverbal and unable to read? While at home, we could dance to Winnie the Pooh songs, and I could read stories to him. Our favorites were *Good Night Moon* and *Brown Bear, Brown Bear, What Do You See?* Adam would intermittently interrupt me with the appropriate next word and be so pleased with himself during story time. At home, he could challenge me to a jumping contest where I undoubtedly would lose, since his stamina was remarkable when he received replacement cortisol. Adam's medical fragility made me appreciate him more and want to do things to make him smile. Away at college, I longed to maintain my relationship with him. I worried that moving away would destroy that connection. I feared many things when it came to Adam. That I might come home and find that he no longer recognized me. That he might start developing behavior problems when I was gone. That he might become progressively more ill or, God forbid, possibly die from another clothes-chute-like incident while I was away. I would be unable to hug him or read him one last story and tell him I loved him. All these fears resonated at the back of my mind.

During winter quarter of my freshman year, I volunteered at Croyden Avenue School, a local school serving individuals with special needs. By my junior year, I had become a part-time employee. My memories of Croyden are fond ones: teaching Bryan, a nine-year-old child with autism, how to tie his shoes ("loop, loop, over, under, pull"); praising Jacob for his flawless drawings of Winnie the Pooh and other Disney characters; hugging a sensory-deprived Shay each time she would tell me in her angelic voice, "I wanna more hugs, please." I saw Adam in every one of the students: every laugh, every smile, every little accomplishment. Adam everywhere. Although I will never be able to be by Adam forever, I know I will continue to foster relationships where I am reminded of him. When I share myself with people with special needs and focus on their abilities rather than their disabilities, I hold on to my relationship with Adam. Thanks to living with and loving Adam, I appreciate life—its fragility and uncertainties. I also appreciate and celebrate small achievements. I open myself to the world. Without Adam, I am not sure if I would be able to do these things at this age. Adam and all his quirks opened my eyes to a world where compassion overcomes fear, where judgment comes after the facts are evaluated, where individuality is valued and encouraged. Adam will always need extra care and protection; I can only hope that he will be surrounded by kindness and tolerance. These underappreciated traits allow life to be more peaceful and happy for all.

* * *

My mother, however, was much older and more experienced than I. Old enough to understand reality, she took the practical route. She collected every towel in the house and put them in the washer with laundry detergent. She took all the freshly washed towels and marched upstairs to her bedroom where she promptly stuffed them down the laundry chute, one by one, to clean up the olive oil. Then, she did the only thing a mother of a child like Adam could do.

She took hammer and nails and nailed that clothes chute shut.

Our Family Has Two Hearts

11

My Older
Sister Ge and I

Helen McCabe and Chuan Wu

We (the authors) have known each other since 1992. We met when Helen was twenty-one, Chuan was three, and her older sister Ge was eight. Though this essay focuses on Chuan's experience as Ge's little sister, we have written it in the form of a dialogue between Helen, Chuan, and the reader. We present it to the reader in this way because it was through an ongoing dialogue as well as the co-writing that this story of autism and sibling experience in the People's Republic of China emerged.

* * *

Chuan: After my sister was diagnosed with autism, my parents despaired at first. No one knew anything about autism in China at that time. They soon found that they had to find their own way to help my sister, to "solve this problem," because there was no one from whom they could learn. It was 1988, and autism had only been diagnosed in China, in our city of Nanjing, for the first time in 1982. There was no information about education for children with autism and, of course, no opportunities. But after six months of total despair, together they determined to do whatever they could for my sister. They wanted to teach her themselves, try to get her into a special-education school if possible, and provide for her as best they could. Well, that is where I come into the story, too. One reason they went from despair to hope was because I came into this world and brought new things to their lives, also to my sister's life. I was born in a country where most families only had one child, so a big reason for them to have a second child was to help my sister in the future. Her name is Zhang Ge; Zhang is her family name, the same as our father's family name. My name is Wu Chuan; I was given my mom's family name. So two of us have the last name "Zhang," and two of us the last name "Wu." By giving me my mother's family name, my parents thought this would change the family, change our luck and bring better things into our lives.

Helen: In all these years knowing each other, being in many ways a part of the Wu and Zhang family, I have never once been told so directly that this name was given to change the family's luck. But it makes sense, and I suppose I suspected it. Autism (and other disabilities) in China are often seen as a punishment for a wrongdoing done by family members. Some families even change the name of the child with autism once he or she is diagnosed, thinking this will have a positive effect on the child. In fact, in Chuan's family, whatever the reason for giving her the surname Wu, her parents indeed fell in despair when Ge was diagnosed. At first, they thought she was a genius because she had unusual and special skills, the earliest being the ability to read most newspapers by age two. Only later did they realize that, though she recognized every character in the dictionary, her comprehension was very limited. Going from the parents of a genius to parents of a child with a lifelong disability, especially a disability that was basically unheard of in China in 1988, was a nightmare. Everyone had envied them, but now people pitied or avoided them. But her parents decided to face facts, strive to teach their daughter as best they could, and to have another child. In this way, her sibling could help Ge when they were old and unable to care for her.

Chuan: In Chinese society, children are the hope of the future. There is an expression, "wangzi chenglong," which means that parents hope their children become dragons. In other words this means that your child will become the most successful, well-respected, and accomplished member in society. But with my sister, it seemed they had "failed" right from the beginning because she would never be what society considers "successful." She would not even have the chance to go to a regular school like other kids, let alone get a PhD or become a scientist or wealthy entrepreneur. To make things even more painful, I have a cousin who is just one month younger than my sister. She is very smart, went to the best high school in our city, and a top university in China. Each time she passed a milestone, each time she accomplished something new, my parents would compare Ge to her and feel sad. While our cousin was preparing for competitive high-school exams, Ge was facing the end of any school (special education) with no job or schooling prospects. They even compared me to my cousin and hoped I would accomplish as much or more than she did. Even though I didn't get into the top high school as she did, I got into a very competitive one, and I have been successful in my journey toward becoming an artist. My accomplishments, both academic and otherwise, have helped my parents to be proud of me and Ge, and the things we have done, even if they are different from what my cousin (who is now pursuing a science PhD) is doing.

Helen: Chuan is a very well-rounded young lady. She is very bright in traditional academic subjects, but she is also a strong leader, an excellent artist (painting), and an outgoing and fun person to be with. In China, being well-rounded isn't the goal—rather, the goal is to do well on high-school- and college-entrance exams, which only measure ability in traditional academics and do so on the basis of the entrance exam alone. At first, her parents hoped that she would be more like her cousin, but later they grew to appreciate both their daughters and the diversity of experiences that came from having Ge and Chuan. They currently are very proud of Chuan's artistic achievements, which she is pursuing while also staying at the top of her college class academically.

Chuan: I was born when my sister was five, and I soon learned that I must take good care of her no matter what happened. My parents always said, "You must take care of Older Sister. She needs your help. You are a smart and capable little sister." I learned to share when I was very young, always dividing treats with her and never hiding anything for myself. In addition, I have always known what "responsibility" means much better than others. I loved playing with her and being the little helper. My parents are glad that I am a girl—they said a younger brother would not have been as good to her.

Helen: Since the late 1970s, China has been implementing a family-planning policy that largely limits families to one child per family. There are various exceptions, including when the first has a disability. Chuan's parents chose this option to have a second child legally and taught Chuan from a very early age that she must be in charge and care for her older sister. Given the social context in China, it is not surprising that Chuan and Ge's parents felt they needed to plan for Ge's future immediately, including having a second child. There is still the general cultural expectation that children will care for their parents in their old age. This is related to the fact that social-welfare provisions for the elderly are very limited, causing the government to assume that each couple will want one child who is healthy and does not have a disability. In this family, Chuan's parents often say, "We don't need Chuan to care for us when we are old; we will pay to live in an old folks' home. We just need to know that Ge will not be alone. Even if Chuan does not live with Ge, she will be alive and able to make sure that Ge is not mistreated or harmed."

Giving birth to a second child when the first has autism is a very controversial subject in China. Part of it is that society has already become accustomed to one-child families and having a second child is clearly outside the norm. Also, some families think this is "unfair" to a second child, to have a child born with a burden on his or her shoulders. In contrast, others think that, in order to do right by their first child, they must have a second child. This was closer to the thinking of Chuan and Ge's parents. Chuan's parents taught her to share, to be responsible, and to be independent throughout her childhood and her life. At age three, because adults were not allowed, she was in charge of helping her eight-year-old sister use the public children's swimming pool, including changing in the locker room and using the pool. Chuan never complained. In fact, she took delight in being the "smart" one, the leader, the teacher.

Chuan: I remember I took Ge swimming when we were kids. In "typical" families, the older sister is the one to take care of and look out for the younger one. But in my family, it was and is the opposite. I told her what to do, and she listened to me. Also, I always saved the best food for my sister, made sure Ge was able to go on rides in the park with me, go shopping, things like that. If one egg was bigger than the other, I would give her the bigger one. It didn't feel like a chore or anything bad, though. It was more like instinct, something I naturally did.

Helen: In fact, Chuan and I agree that this background has helped her succeed in school—where she has been a class leader since preschool, always organizing events, helping the teachers, etc. But maybe it has been stressful, too.

Chuan: No. Not stressful. First, I also remember that Ge was a good big sister to me in some ways. My parents tell me the story about how, before I was born, Ge always liked to poke the dolls' eyes. Mom and Dad were afraid she would do the same to me, so they told her time and time again, "She is your younger sister; you can't poke her eyes!" It seems that Ge understood this; she did not poke my eyes but was gentle with me. What's more, sometimes when I fell down, she would pick me up and give me to my mother, saying, "Little sister fell down." Plus, my parents have always supported me and allowed me opportunities to succeed in school and in life. I have been the class leader (class monitor) throughout high school. I was the leader of different committees in middle school. I was class representative for the science classes in high school. Even if that took extra time at school, my parents supported me and allowed me to do it, so I could develop to my fullest potential. Helen asked me before what the difference is between my family and other families in China. It's simple. Other families have one heart, one core (重心 zhongxin); our family has two hearts, two cores—that is, me and Ge.

Helen: When Chuan first used this expression with me, two hearts (or two cores), I felt that I finally understood her experience and her beliefs. Was it possible that she never felt stressed at being so different, at having a sister with autism in a society with so little awareness, tolerance, and so few services? Why didn't she feel angry about all the responsibility placed on her? But given that I have been very close to her whole family for seventeen years, when she explained it this way, I immediately understood exactly what she meant. Chuan and Ge's parents love and provide support and encouragement to both daughters. While some families in China fear that, if they have a second child, the first child with autism will be neglected, this family never even considered this problem. They were not having a second child to "replace" the first one, but rather to join the family, to complete the family. Over the years, the focus of both parents has been on both children. Their mother left her work when Ge graduated from special-education school at the age of fifteen. Their father passed up opportunities for better work and higher salary in order to have more time to spend with both girls. And the result? Parents who share responsibility, two children who are loved and know that they are, truly, the hearts and cores of the family.

Chuan. Right. The main difference between us and other families in China is that a lot of families have just one child. But I feel that otherwise we are a "normal" family. For me, from my earliest memories, I began to realize that I was different from others. But it was about the number of people in our family. I would see the other families at school, just two parents and one child. But we were two parents and two children.

Helen: Still, it is difficult to be "different" in China. Individuals with disability and their families are often looked down on, laughed at, mistreated. There is so little information and understanding of difference of any kind among many people in society. Many families of children with autism have told me about people talking behind their backs and telling them they should not take their child out of the house, as well as of the difficulty of getting a child accepted into school. Many children with autism are turned away both from general-education schools and special-education schools because teachers are simply not trained and feel that autism is not their responsibility. This is changing slowly, with a new major in autism being introduced at Nanjing Technical College of Special Education, the first of its kind in China, and with the growing number of organizations providing intervention due to the growing number of individuals diagnosed with autism. While Chuan may not have felt a lot of this discrimination, it affected her parents, certainly.

Chuan: I suppose in some ways it was more difficult. And you know, it wasn't just having two children versus one. It's not like twins, who might be double the work but are very similar to each other. Instead, my parents could not use the same ways to teach Ge and me. Ge needed more time than I did to learn things. But on the other hand, it was harder to educate me, too—I mean, to educate me about Ge. How much can you expect a child really to understand about disability, about autism? I learned gradually, though.

Helen: Communication in Chinese families is very indirect. This family is no exception. Whenever I talk to Chuan or her parents about how she learned about autism or even that her sister had autism, they all say it happened gradually and naturally. Rather than sitting Chuan down one day and explaining autism, she slowly started to hear the word *autism*, including those times when I was at their house. Because they were getting to know this foreigner from the U.S. who had an interest in autism, the disability was a natural topic of conversation around the house. Through overhearing our discussions and those of other families of children with autism who came over to share experiences and seek guidance, Chuan started to grasp that Ge had something called autism (*gudu zheng*). She has learned quite a bit through just listening to people talking, both at home and in more public places like television interviews.

Chuan: I cannot tell what happened before I came into the world, but I know it was difficult for my parents. I have learned from interviews they have done with newspapers and television programs they have been on. But still, I can only feel one percent of the bitterness they have undergone. For me, I have seen people staring at Ge, giving her funny looks. Sometimes when I was younger and riding on the bus, if someone looked at her funny, I would glare at that person until the person got embarrassed and stopped. Just recently, we were together with my parents and Ge at the bus stop. Ge was crying because she was upset about something that happened earlier that day, and all those people were looking at us.

Helen: I remember that. I was angry that they were staring and sad that Ge was upset. I was also proud of you for the way you responded to and consoled your older sister.

Chuan: We take care of each other. When I used to come home each night from high school (up until this past year; now I am in college in the U.S.), Ge would come to meet me at the bus stop and offer to carry my heavy bag. I didn't always let her. I don't want to take advantage of her! But it was nice to be picked up by someone, especially when it was dark out and late at night. I like being with her. She gives everyone in our family nicknames. She is "big face cat," and I am "little face cat" [from a cartoon in China]. We get along well, and she likes when I am with her, too. Even though she doesn't tell me directly how she feels, I know she is happy with me, and we just know how each other is feeling.

Helen: Chuan told me once that most of her friends and people at school had no idea she had a sister with autism. I was surprised. How do you keep something like that hidden from everyone?

Chuan: It's true. Up through high school, I had two identities in my life. At school, I was Chuan, a good artist, a strong student, a class leader. My classmates and I did not really talk to each other about our families, and we did not spend time at classmates' homes. We talked about friends, about classes, about school activities; but I did not have much interaction with classmates outside school. This was not unusual—many of my classmates are like that. The main reason is that we had to study all the time, to prepare for the high school and, later, the university entrance exams. We did not have time to hang out at each others' homes. In high school, I was usually in school, including evening study hall, until 8 p.m., and it was almost 10 p.m. by the time I returned home. Who would have time to get to know each other's families and home lives? Besides, I knew they would not understand, because it was too unusual to have a sister with autism. Since they wouldn't understand, I did not want to bother to tell them. However, outside school, I have always been known as "Ge's sister." Especially on television programs and newspaper articles, I am always introduced as "Ge's little sister." And actually, now that I am in college in the United States, when my friends ask me about my family, I do tell them about having a sister with autism. I tell them because they can understand. Autism is more well known in the U.S.—when I tell my friends about Ge, many times they will say to me, "Oh, my brother has autism, too" or "Oh, my cousin has autism." Something like this would never happen in China!

Helen: The media attention to this family has been considerable in China. Chuan's family is quite well known among families and professionals involved with autism in that country. Ge was diagnosed very early (1988, just six years after autism was first diagnosed), so she is one of the oldest people *known* to have autism in China. Of course, there are many others much older than her (she is now twenty-five), but they largely have had incorrect diagnoses or never received a diagnosis. Chuan's parents were fortunate to be living in Nanjing, the city where autism was first diagnosed in 1982 by Dr. Tao Kuo-tai. This helped them to get an appropriate diagnosis before age four. Since that time, they never hid their daughter's diagnosis, which is still common in China today. There is still a lot of discrimination and stigma in China against people with disabilities, including autism, which is still so little understood there. This, not surprisingly, causes many families to hide their children, hide their diagnosis. But after a six-month period of complete despair (during which they did not hide the diagnosis but did not actively seek solutions), Chuan's family was much more proactive, letting others know Ge had autism as they sought out educational opportunities for her. This openness led to many media outlets learning of their situation and seeking them out for interviews, especially since 2002 when Ge was eighteen years old and her parents were seeking vocational opportunities for her, including volunteering.

Chuan: I was on television in 2002 for the program where they tried to find my sister a job. They got her a temporary volunteer position at a grocery store, but the store said they didn't need her when that trial period was up. So it wasn't helpful in that way, but it helped to get more attention to autism and to her needs as a young adult with autism. At that time, I was in the sixth grade, and it was so much fun to be in the television studio, go up on the stage with the hosts and everyone. They even had a birthday cake for Ge because the filming was right around her birthday. But honestly, after that time, I was busy in school, and I also started to get annoyed at reporters asking me the same questions over and over. I started to avoid reporters and refused to be interviewed. I said, "It has nothing to do with me, and besides, haven't you already asked these questions before?" But I understand why my parents are willing to be on television. They want more people to know about autism, and this will make people in our community and around China pay more attention to the disorder and may lead to more help for people with autism. So this makes sense to me now, even though I didn't want to be on television myself.

Helen: Between 2002 and 2008, the media has indeed been very active in seeking out stories about this family; as Chuan said, the content does get repetitive. The main idea in most of these reports is that these parents have sacrificed so much, their careers, etc., in order to advocate for their daughter with autism. Their story is seen as an inspiration for others, and it also has been helpful in getting the word out regarding autism. Some families read about them and realize, for the first time, what is "different" about their own child. Still, the content does feel repetitive, but for newly diagnosed families, it is useful. Interestingly, this family and the media surrounding them was nominated once for "The Ten Most Moving Stories of 2004" and then later selected as one of the "Top 100 Happiest Families in China." They are a success story.

Chuan: The success story sometimes involves me! When other parents of children with autism find out that I am Ge's sister and that I am now attending a competitive college in the U.S., they are often amazed and say, "Wow, your parents have accomplished so much despite so much difficulty! They have done more than twice what other parents have done!" My success in school, my sister's success in her life, all this makes me proud to be her sister, to be known as "Ge's sister." I mean, when people proudly say, "This is Ge's sister," I know they are also thinking about how my sister is doing, and I feel happy about that. She has a job now at our community library; it's rare to have this kind of job, maybe even a first in China! It means that what my parents have worked so hard for over the past twenty years, for the success of us two "hearts" of the family, has been accomplished!

Helen: Getting back to Chuan's two identities...

Chuan: Right. So up to recently, no one at school knew I had a sister with autism. In China, most families have just one child, so no one even knew I had a sister or sibling at all. But then in spring 2008, we were all on television, my family and I and Helen; our experiences together over the years were the subject of the program *Zhou Tao Tells Stories*. About ten friends and teachers of mine saw it, and they were so surprised! They said that I am Chuan in their minds, yet one day they learned that I am also "Ge's sister." I have this whole other identity. My art teacher said he had no idea I even had a sister at all! From the television program, he learned that I am not only a class leader, but I am also a caring and responsible younger sister of a young woman with autism. He was impressed with my character and wished me well in my future, including study in the U.S.

Helen: Deciding to come to the U.S. for higher education was a decision that we all made together. I may have been more hesitant than anyone, even though it was actually my idea. I raised the possibility and offered some advice along the way. But I was unsure how each family member would handle this, especially Ge and Chuan. Plus, Chuan was brought up knowing she should care for her sister. But in college in the U.S., she would be unable directly to help at all. I know that is a selfish concern on my part, meaning I was thinking too much about Ge and not about Chuan, but I have to be honest.

Chuan: But even if I went to university in China, I would not be home as much as when I was in high school. Besides, this is temporary and is an opportunity to change my future, improve my future. That means improving Ge's future, too. She will always live with me: that is the plan, and it is what I want. But by studying in the U.S., I can get a better job when I return to China.

Helen: Actually, Chuan's parents don't necessarily want Ge to live with her. As we talked about and wrote this essay, I told Chuan this. Of course, the sisters living together would make their parents feel secure, but they know Chuan should have her own life. It wasn't always like that, of course. At first, the future they saw was Ge living with Chuan, maybe helping around the house and being a part of Chuan's own family after she married. There was no other possibility. But as Chuan got older, her parents realized that this expectation was not fair. They still expect Chuan to be close to Ge and provide whatever support might be needed in the future, but they hope that there will be other support for Ge, too, such as her older cousin who lives nearby and has been very generous and caring to Ge over the years. Of course, this doesn't mean Ge will live with him either. The future details are still uncertain. Social services for individuals with disabilities are still very limited in China, especially for older children and adults. There are no group homes or other residential placements for Chuan's parents to look forward to for the future. However, there have been extensive reforms in China over the past thirty years, including reforms in education and special education, and there is some cautious optimism that this may positively impact adults with autism in the future.

Chuan: Many people in China see having a child with a disability as a punishment for something they did wrong. But when it happens to a family, it just feels so unfair. "Why me?" is what they think. So it is interesting that a lot of neighbors, when they know about me, they say to my parents, "The gods are fair. You have a daughter with autism, but you also have another daughter, Chuan, who has brought you a different kind of experience and happiness as a parent." This is true for my parents, but they also get a feeling of joy and satisfaction from my sister Ge.

Helen: Chuan knows her family is special in some ways, and she is proud of what they have accomplished. What she said about her parents getting feelings of joy from her sister too is also something that I hear a lot from her parents. When people ask them (as they often do), "But really, who is your favorite daughter?," they say "You just don't understand. They are completely different people. We love them both, equally, but our relationships with them are different. You can't compare it, measure it." This fits with Chuan's talking about her family having two hearts, and it's the way we all see this family, our family.

Robie

Erika Reich Giles

12

My brother Robie was twenty-eight years old when he died. After dinner on June 29, 1977, at the Boulder River School and Hospital in Boulder, Montana, he choked to death. A regurgitated string bean. That's what the staff doctor told Mom when he called. Sobbing, she relayed the news to me in Seattle. An autopsy confirmed the cause of death. I imagine Robie sitting on his bed in his dormitory, his lanky body crumpling as he gasped for air and no one noticing. For a long time, I couldn't even look at string beans. Avoiding string beans was all I had left to try to compensate—for my embarrassment, my neglect, my reluctance to acknowledge to others his existence for most of his life. At the same time, I considered him almost my twin, born exactly one year and one day after me, his sister.

Robie was two years old when unknown forces began to rob him of his developing speech, to cause his mind to regress and turn inward. We were living in Rohrbach, Austria, his birthplace, a village nestled in the foothills of the Alps. Three years earlier, in 1948, my parents, my five-year-old sister Judy, and I, cradled in my mother's arms, had escaped from Soviet-occupied Communist Hungary as the borders were being sealed. Did my parents, struggling to build a new life, realize at first what was happening to Robie? Perhaps the process was so gradual that they could deny for a time that anything was wrong. Or perhaps they were preoccupied with fears of the Soviets, who, as part of the Allied partitioning of Austria after World War II, controlled a sector of the country only five miles away. Concerns were widespread that they would try to grab even more territory. My parents resolved to put that threat permanently behind us. In 1952, we emigrated to the United States as refugees, settling in Billings, Montana, an arid town of 50,000 on the western edge of the Great Plains.

By then, we all knew that Robie, a cute, chubby-cheeked boy of three, was different, an impression heightened by the passage of time. "Kong...kong...kong," he intoned in a sing-song voice, flapping his hands and forearms in excitement. Sometimes, his face and arms turned rigid, his eyes staring in apprehension at a threat only he could see. Or he burst into gales of laughter at jokes evident only to himself. He scribbled aimlessly on sheets of typing paper with pencils or crayon. Few toys interested him. But he was fascinated with a set of flat, wooden tiles—red, yellow, blue, green, purple—and used them to create intricate designs that a family friend marveled at even years later. And he loved trains: wooden trains that he pulled along the edge of our yellow Formica kitchen table and passenger and freight trains rolling on the rails bisecting our town. Robie erupted with "choo-haha, choo-haha" whenever a train whistle blared. He was restless, often in motion. On the rare occasion that he sat still, he never looked directly at anyone, not even us. Instead, he gazed beyond our faces, as though foreseeing a future that didn't include us.

Mom, petite and attractive, with hair the color of dark chocolate cascading down her back, understood Robie best. Talkative and bursting with energy, she also had a volatile temper. But she was always patient with Robie, instinctively anticipating his wants and needs. His vulnerability aroused in her a fierce, protective love. Pony-tailed Judy, with wide, blue eyes, preferred spending time with her friends to babysitting Robie and me while Mom cleaned rooms at Deaconess Hospital and Dad fabricated sheet metal at Eaton's. But she, too, reserved her gentler side for Robie. He gravitated toward her and Mom, allowing them to hold and caress him all they wanted. Dad, as reserved as Mom was outgoing, was tall and slender, a handsome man with dark hair combed sideways over a high forehead. He was a perfectionist and liked order in his life. Robie, so different from the son he must have imagined to carry on the family name, bewildered him. He remained in the background. And I, similar in appearance to Robie but taller, so close in age and too young to understand fully, just accepted him as part of the landscape of my childhood.

Most of my memories of Robie are embodied in photographs, individual moments frozen in time, black-and-white photographs with white, serrated edges stored in Mom's albums on a brick-and-board bookcase in my former bedroom. Like an artist's tint, memory supplies the hues. The earliest photographs, before he left home, are in a green album with an edelweiss on the cover. Several burgundy albums, their vinyl covers bordered in gold, hold the photos from his twenty-two years in the institution.

Summer 1952. Robie, in a gingham shirt and rompers, clutches the chains of a swing in the yard of our first Billings house, on Rimrock Road, near the sandstone cliffs dominating the town's north side. Blue eyes squint against the sun. His hair, flaxen like mine, flops over his forehead in a "V." Always eager for a ride, he looks like he's waiting for someone to push him.

April 1955. Robie and I sit side by side at a table covered with a white cloth and Mom's good china decorated with lilies of the valley. Our hair is darker; our bodies are skinny. We are in the cramped kitchen of our Avenue E house, part of a project originally built for families of soldiers returning from World War II. Two gift-wrapped packages. His bulky, perhaps a truck. Mine flat, probably a book. Six candles adorn a Hungarian *dobos torta*, a yellow cake with chocolate frosting, and seven are on a chocolate pie, edged in whipped cream. We both smile at the camera, but Robie rests his chin on his plate. It is our last birthday together.

A few months later, Robie and I were home alone one afternoon, locked in the house with strict orders not to go out or let anyone in. We might have been sitting on the floor, playing with his tiles, when he suddenly stood up and rushed to the door. He struggled to turn the knob of the deadbolt. "No, Robie," I shouted, jumping up and pulling him away. Perhaps I succeeded in distracting him for a while with his wooden train. But the door was a magnet. Again, I tugged on his arm. He was smaller than I was, but determination made him stronger. We struggled until, finally, he thrust me aside, opened the door, and raced down the street. "Come back, Robie," I yelled. He ignored me. I knew it was useless to follow, that I could never catch him. It didn't occur to me to try to get help. Instead, I slouched into the house and waited, fearful of what would happen to him—and to me for letting him go.

My parents must have been upset when they returned, but the focus would not have been on me but on finding Robie. The police were called. Eventually, Robie, wrapped in an olive-drab army blanket, emerged from a police cruiser in front of our house, oblivious to the agitation he had caused. The officers had found him wandering more than a mile away, at the Evergreen Shopping Center. Naked. His clothes were scattered on the streets where he had shed them. I was relieved that he was safe, that my parents didn't blame me. But I blamed myself. And I felt a new emotion—embarrassment. For him. For all of us.

That day when Robie was six, reality collided with hope. Two years earlier, Mom had taken him to a child psychologist. Her friend Angela, a fellow Hungarian refugee, more fluent in English, acted as an interpreter. At the end of the testing, Angela, without preamble, translated the psychologist's diagnosis: "Your son is an idiot." The term was part of the classification system for levels of mental retardation in use at the time. Only in hindsight, with more information, have we realized that Robie was, in fact, autistic. Perhaps, only ten years after autism's discovery in 1943, the psychologist hadn't yet heard about the diagnosis. And even if he had, what could he have offered when, even now, the disorder is in many ways a mystery?

The diagnosis devastated my parents. Still, they did everything possible to try to shelter Robie within our family. But with his latest escapade, they were forced to acknowledge that they couldn't manage his behavior, that he needed more supervision than they could provide. The only option was the Montana State Training School in Boulder, 250 miles away.

Spring 1957. Mom, in a navy-blue coat with a white shawl collar, stands with Robie in front of a brick building on the school grounds. Holding his hand, she gazes down at him. He, small and vulnerable-looking in a jacket and knitted cap, rests his face on her sleeve. For a long time, I thought the photograph was taken the day Mom and Jackie, our refugee sponsor, moved him there. It was actually months later. I imagine a similar scene on his first day. Smiling, Mom would have held Robie close, putting on a brave front, though her heart must have been breaking. And he, trusting, would have grasped her hand, unaware that she was leaving him and would not return for a very long time.

Did he cry that night on his narrow metal bed in a row of beds filled with strangers? Did he wonder what had happened, why she had left him? How many days or weeks or months passed before he realized that this was his new home? Mom, always private, never said what it was like to say goodbye to her youngest child, only six years old. I didn't ask. I was relieved that he was gone, that there would be no more embarrassing incidents, that I could invite friends home without having to explain what was wrong with my little brother.

My parents visited Robie two or three times a year, usually when the tug of that invisible line connecting him to Mom's heart became unbearable to her. Sometimes, Judy and I joined them. Or just I did. We would have visited more often, but spending two nights in a motel was a luxury my parents, still struggling to find their financial footing in our adopted country, could ill afford. With each visit, my mother, who by then worked six days a week cleaning houses, lost two days of pay. And the trip on two-lane highways took five hours—longer in winter, if the roads were even passable—confining most of our visits to warmer months.

Dad drove our 1955 Chevrolet sedan or his panel truck from Billings across arid flatlands to Lavina, west to White Sulphur Springs, through the Big Belt Mountains to Townsend, past Canyon Ferry Lake to Helena, Montana's capital, and finally, high into the forested Elkhorn Mountains to Boulder.

It was a sleepy town set in a wide valley, best known for the school and for hot springs and radon mines where people sought relief from arthritis, gout, and bursitis. The institution was on the far side of downtown, stretching over several acres along the shallow Boulder River. A half-dozen early 1900s two-story, red-brick buildings surrounded by lawns and trees served as the facility's headquarters and dormitories for hundreds of residents. Low, modern structures housed a school and hospital. In the background were maintenance buildings, industrial shops, warehouses. Crossing over a bridge leading to the entrance, we wound slowly down the drive, past a sign reminding us, "Our Children Have the Right of Way," past an occasional resident sitting in a wheelchair on a porch or walking down the road. If they waved, I, though suddenly shy, waved back. Dad pulled up to Robie's dormitory, "Aspen," and Mom got out of the car to fetch him. Sometimes, she asked me to join her. As we waited in the large entryway, boys crowded around, greeting us, touching us. There were too many of them and they came too close and they talked too loud and I was scared. But I tried not to show it. After all, they were like my brother. But I was always glad when Robie arrived and, after we greeted him with hugs and kisses, the three of us could leave.

For most of the eight or nine years I visited Robie with my parents, he looked like a child. Thin, undersized, he was always shorter than I was. His hair, cropped close, emphasized protruding ears. He didn't talk. But he did respond to simple commands, even in Hungarian. He grimaced more. His movements—the flapping of his hands and arms—were more frantic. The sounds he made—especially "kong…kong…kong"— were louder. Or did it just seem that way to me because I was no longer accustomed to Robie?

We stayed at the O-Z Motel, a white, concrete-block structure with six or seven units facing North Main Street. Red-brick buildings, some dating to the town's origin in the 1880s, surrounded it on the wide thoroughfare tapering to dust at the edge of the asphalt. The Lounge and one or two other bars were the most prominent businesses. On rare occasions, my parents splurged for the Diamond S Ranch Hotel, a stodgy place three miles south of town, with a hot springs pool. But things were simpler, less embarrassing at the O-Z. The manager, a jean-clad woman in her thirties with a friendly smile and short, brown hair, was accustomed to seeing residents from the school, and we avoided crossing a lobby with people who stared at Robie.

We strolled around town on unpaved side streets with large trees, past clapboard houses, the turreted Jefferson County Courthouse, the white-frame Catholic church, a barren hill with the town's silver water tower. We took turns holding Robie's hands, so he couldn't run away. On nice days, we picnicked on the banks of the icy Boulder River, eating meals Mom prepared at home and packed in our green-metal Coleman cooler: potato salad, bologna sandwiches on white bread, apples, oranges, Hungarian lattice-topped bar cookies, rácsos tészta, filled with strawberry jam.

But we spent most of the time in our room. A double bed, a rollaway, a Formica table, a couple of vinyl-covered chairs, a ceramic lamp. Drab shades of beige and brown. Off the main space, a kitchenette and a tiny bathroom with a shower. Within those walls, Mom compressed months of mothering into a few hours. She bathed Robie, brushed his teeth, combed his hair, fussed with his clothes, fed him, held him on her lap. He became real to me again during those visits, a flesh-and-blood brother instead of a memory growing dimmer. But I usually felt awkward, unsure of how to act, what to do. Like Dad and Judy, I hovered on the periphery, letting Mom take the lead, giving her precious time with Robie. For a couple of days, we could pretend that our family was whole again.

Summer 1959. Robie stands next to the river on a cloudy day, wearing denim overalls and a dark sport coat. Not his clothes. His mouth is twisted into a grimace. Perhaps this was the visit that Mom discovered bruises on his back. She and Dad complained to the superintendent, and the counselor responsible was reportedly fired.

Spring 1961. Robie and I sit at the foot of pine trees in the city park. We're wearing Austrian clothes, birthday gifts from Omama, our paternal grandmother in Austria. He, in a forest-green jacket and a jaunty green-and-white hat, slumps against me, his legs crossed. In my red-and-white checked dress and white apron, I grasp his shoulders. It looks like I'm trying to hold him up.

What did he think of our visits? When he had given up hope, when he finally accepted that he was being left, did it confuse him to have us reappear for a couple of days, only to disappear again? Did he even remember us? There must have come a point that we became the strangers, and the counselors and his fellow residents became his family. The hardest part was not being able to communicate. Not knowing what he thought. Not knowing what he felt.

For the first few years after Robie went to Boulder, I believed he would get better. After all, he was at a "training school," which, to my child's mind, implied that he would learn things, maybe even start to talk. My best friend Joan shared my optimism. Her brother Dennis, a stocky, dark-haired boy Robie's age, had a speech impediment and was making progress in therapy. Joan and I planned how our brothers, mirroring us, would play together when Robie came home. I don't know when I realized it was only a fantasy, that Robie wasn't coming back. But gradually, we stopped discussing that possibility. When I was in sixth grade, my family moved, and I transferred to another school. Joan's and my friendship ended.

After that, I avoided talking about Robie. I was sure, if people knew, they would make fun of him, or of me. Like the time our neighbor Billy, a year or two older, with straw-colored hair and bad skin, sneered that he'd heard I had a brother who couldn't talk. Or when my cousin Suzie, in a group of friends, imitated a retarded person, stumbling over her words and lurching around. She might not have been thinking of Robie, but I was shattered. In eighth-grade speech class, I had no choice but to mention Robie in my autobiography; it was being recorded, and I would receive a shiny black disk to play for my parents. I mumbled a reference to his birth, hoping my classmates wouldn't notice. To my relief, no one did. I dreaded questions about siblings, and when anyone asked, I told them I had an older sister. But not mentioning Robie always felt wrong—as if each time I denied his existence, he was being diminished, like the fading of a photograph.

In high school, I went along on fewer visits to Robie. I was busy with classes, homework, Activity Club, church choir, an after-school clerical job with three doctors. All provided a convenient excuse to avoid confronting the maturation of Robie's body while his mind stood still. I could also avoid the guilt and discomfort I felt with my growing realization that, given our closeness in age, our situations could easily have been reversed.

July 1963. Robie sits between Judy and me on a large boulder in pants that are too short and a plaid shirt revealing painfully skinny arms. Judy is twenty, I am fifteen, and Robie fourteen. None of us is smiling. It is the last photograph of us together.

* * *

At Macalester College in St. Paul, Minnesota, I rarely thought about Robie. So far from home, it was even easier not to talk about him. Mom mentioned him occasionally—as when she and Dad, driving to pick him up at the renamed Boulder River School and Hospital, found him, by then a boy-man, squatting in the road on a chilly day. He wasn't wearing underwear, and his jacket wasn't warm enough.

One Christmas after college, I decided to send him a gift. Guessing his size, I selected a navy-blue wool, v-necked sweater and wrapped it as I had watched my mother do all those years that she had enclosed her love in packages wrapped in brown paper and secured with twine. Packages with socks, underwear, shirts, pants, toy trains and trucks, and cellophane bags of soft, orange "peanuts" that he could chew and hard candies and caramels to be shared. I chose a bright red-and-green card, maybe with a picture of Santa Claus, and signed it, "With love, from your sister." He would not have known who it was from or the depth of feeling it carried, even after all that time. Despite my embarrassment, my neglect, and my silence, I did love him. I loved him, and I wished we'd had a different life, a life in which we had grown up together, a life in which I would have thought him a pest but tolerated him, and we would have argued and made up, and I would have taught him things, and we would have compared notes about my boyfriends and his girlfriends, and we would have stood up for each other and been each other's best friend.

Instead, Robie became a stranger. In a photograph in my parents' bedroom, taken shortly before he died, his pale skin is stretched over an angular face with a high forehead topped by dark brown, wavy hair. He is wearing a grayish-green sweater, the long fingers of his hands touching in front of him. His blue eyes are vacant, devoid of even the slightest spark. There is a suggestion of a bruise on his face.

Every year when I visit my parents in Billings, we go to the plot in Mountview Cemetery where Robie's ashes are buried. There is a small bronze plaque with his name and the years spanning his life: 1949–1977. Mom and Dad will eventually join him there, on a rise overlooking the grayish, barren hills beyond the Yellowstone River. I'd like to think his spirit is hovering nearby. I'd like to think he forgives me.

His Little Sister

13

Cara Murphy Watkins

In the Great Lakes region of upstate New York, winters are interminable and played out under a low, solid gray sky. It's a world of white for months, not "Winter Wonderland" white but monochromatic and dim. You can measure the days by the age of the snow: the dirty, brown-fringed stuff that's been there for months or the glittering cotton snow falling at the moment.

One brittle, subzero February morning when I was eleven, I was working in our garage with my brother Tim, fifteen. Fresh snow had fallen during the night, topping off a foot of accumulation already on the ground, and the still-falling snow was piling up in drifts as high as the roofs of some cars. The radio in the garage played "Evil Woman" by the Electric Light Orchestra and "Love Will Keep Us Together" by the Captain and Tennille and aired frostbite advisories, reminding listeners that skin exposed to the elements was likely to freeze. It was still dark, just before 5 a.m. and the coldest time of day.

Tim and I were putting together the Sunday newspaper for our shared paper-delivery route. This involved inserting the thick section of comics and advertising pages into the main body of the paper. It was time-consuming, but since our garage was well lit and heated for an attached greenhouse, we were comfortable enough to remove our gloves, scarves, and hats. The paper was so heavy on Sundays that we had split the route in two sections. This way we could carry all the newspapers we needed and not have to circle back and get more.

Tim and I got along okay for siblings: sometimes we fought, sometimes we cooperated. Mostly we ignored each other. We had two older brothers, Ed and Terry, both of whom were a lot nicer to Tim and me than Tim and I were to each other.

We fought that morning about who would get the easiest part of the route. Our neighborhood layout was shaped like a bottom-heavy figure 8. The top half, where we lived, we called the Little Block. The bottom half was the Big Block. There was no way fairly to divide up the route. The Little Block was a bit easier, and usually we just took turns; but neither one of us wanted to be out in the cold any longer than necessary that morning.

The argument took its usual course: quickly we were fighting not about the paper route but just sniping at each other about whatever would be most hurtful, something at which I was particularly gifted. To make things more awful, I started singing to the radio. Tim hated it if I—or anyone—sang to the radio.

Tim became so mad he stormed out, sprinting off into the darkness. I didn't give it much thought other than to take a moment to invent and rehearse an excuse in case Tim told our mom. I resigned myself to expect some kind of punishment later and went off to deliver papers to the Little Block.

But nearly an hour later, after I finished my half of the route, I noticed Tim's share of the newspapers still sitting in the garage. It was so cold that the inside of my nose hurt. The temperature was now five degrees and the snow had stopped, but the wind chill factor brought it to ten below zero. I went inside the house thinking Tim was going to make me do his half of the route as revenge, but he hadn't come home. By this time, the night sky was fading into the grayness that passed for daylight.

I was a tiny bit worried. It was slightly possible something had happened to Tim; if it had, it would be my fault. I refilled the newspaper bag and headed back out to finish Tim's half of the route. I hoped he would be home once I was done.

By 7 a.m., Tim hadn't returned. Uncharacteristically, I was worried more about him than about me, so I woke up Mom, something no one ever did lightly. Over the years, I learned that the best way to do this was to wake her up by telling her whatever I had to say and then to get back out into the hallway as quickly as possible and answer any questions from there. Somehow a tongue-lashing always hurt less from a distance. My parents had been divorced since I was five, so as far as the habits of parents went, I thought this was standard maternal behavior, not unlike the handling of beehives, for example.

I told her that Tim had been gone for two hours. It wasn't until I scampered into the hallway that I realized she had said not one word. Instead, she got right out of bed and put on her enormous winter bathrobe, which I thought of as a Pendleton cloud, all white and sky-blue. Then she went downstairs, put on her winter coat (an ankle-length, brown, quilted down jacket that reminded me of a life raft) and some snow boots and walked outside. She just stood in the driveway, peering off into the smeary grayness, looking at nothing I could make out, hoping for Tim to materialize out of snow-burdened evergreens, I guessed, or from behind the claw-branched brown trees. The muffled quiet world of snow all around us seemed deafening while I waited for her to say something. She turned to look down the steep slope of our driveway, making the snow squeak and crunch as she moved. I supposed that if one of my older brothers had been home, she would have sent him out to look for Tim. I offered what I hoped was a helpful comment. "His hat and gloves are on the garage floor," I said. "No one could stand to be out in this too long without them."

She turned—squeak, crunch—and looked at me. The snow had begun to fall again and fat, unmelted flakes were standing like goose down on her short, blond hair. I expected the angry face, the Christ-Almighty-I'm-going-to-brain-you face; instead, my mother's worried expression unsettled me. Anxiety was a rare emotion for her to show. She never seemed like she didn't know what to do.

"Being cold doesn't motivate Tim to do something," she said, turning away and scanning the distance again. "*That* pain doesn't affect him the way it does you or me."

I became very uneasy and filled with shame. Mom almost never pointedly reminded us how Tim was different.

* * *

I grew up knowing that Tim had autism. The philosophy of my mother, as well as Tim's doctors, was that Tim should be treated—within reason—like all kids. He didn't need to be burdened by the label of his impairment and the idea that he required special treatment. Mom felt Tim's quality of life hinged on his confidence. If he was confident in his interactions with people, they were likely to give him the respect he deserved. She was determined to teach Tim not just the skills that we all need to grow up but also to nurture in him the independence that he would need to live on his own one day. At that time, the late 1960s and early 1970s, this treatment of autism was fairly revolutionary; in fact *any* treatment for autism was revolutionary. Most people had never even heard the term.

I grew up taking Tim for granted just as I took for granted my two other brothers. I, of all people, treated Tim exactly as I did everyone else, meaning *not very well*. To me, *autism* was a word like *diabetic* or *nearsighted*. There was even a time when I mentally characterized the people I knew by their differences. The boy next door had diabetes and required an insulin injection each day. The boy on the other side had Down syndrome. The boy behind us had some form of mental disability that didn't have a convenient label. At least two other older boys in the neighborhood—well into their twenties actually—had unlabeled problems and would live at home with their parents their whole lives. One traveled the neighborhood in a golf cart, which was an object of serious envy for me, and the other drove around the streets in his red '74 Camaro and called out through a speaker inside the front grille.

I had my own burdensome differences. My hands sweated constantly and dripped, repulsing most people and making the school papers on which I wrote crinkly. I was painfully shy, yet if something was forbidden me, I seemed compelled to do it and later to lie about it. I was destructive and disrespectful. Most adults found me intolerable.

Everyone had differences of varying extremes, and Tim's were more obvious and numerous, well known and taken for granted by me. I knew he would yell at me and clamp his hands over his ears if I sang to the radio and that there was little sense in arguing with him over television channels—he got his way because he was immune to reason or negotiation and because he was bigger and stronger than I was.

He had no compunction about walking up to people and asking odd personal questions. He made obsessive lists of all the contestants on *Bowling for Dollars* and wrote down all the commercials that ran during *Jeopardy*. He went to a special school that I remember as chaotic and incomprehensible.

When I teased Tim or was mean to him, it was never about his impairment; it was about mundane things. If we were eating lasagna for dinner, for example, I'd tell him that we were eating our next-door neighbors, whose last name, improbably, was Lasagna. "I just ate Christopher's head!" I'd say, chewing my food with unbridled delight. He'd look shocked, drop his fork, and point at me, speechless, and finally yell, "Ahhhhhh, Cara! Mom!"

* * *

Uncharacteristically for a boy with autism, by twelve, my brother Tim had become bold socially. Without hesitation, he would approach anyone and ask his or her name. Usually his targets had something to do with one of his then-current obsessions: utility workers or bald men.

Tim would stand beneath towering utility lines in our neighborhood while he waited for the hard-hatted worker to climb down. Then he'd interview the person. He'd ask—very politely but with some sense of urgency—who the man was, who he worked for, his job title, and how many phones he happened to have in his own home.

"Mr. Miller, are your telephones dial or push-button?"

"They're all dial so far," Mr. Miller would answer.

"And what color are they?"

"Um, let's see, there's the black one, and there's one that's kind of tan in the kitchen."

And then, Tim would conclude things by summing up. "Two dial telephones, one black, one tan, in the Miller household."

At home, the topic of phones was always worthy of a pop quiz.

"Cara, we have how many telephones in our house?" he'd probe, knowing full well the answer.

Six," I'd say, tired of this. "All dial."

"And the colors and locations?"

"Sun porch—black, kitchen—tan, breakfast room—brown, mom's room—tan, third floor—black."

"And," Tim would prompt, "Laundry room?"

"Laundry room—red."

"And what about the Nichols's house?"

But sometimes the questions posed of strangers were a bit more personal. Shiny bald heads were another one of Tim's obsessions. Typically, I'd be going with Tim into the local drugstore when I'd hear this behind me: "Excuse me, sir." Tim was speaking to a man whose head was completely bald. And the man had to be *completely* bald; going bald, combed-over domes, or fringe around the circumference of the head didn't count as bald.

"What's your name, sir?"

I would stop and wait for Tim, rather than go into the store alone. Most people were polite and indulgent. "I'm Jack Baker. And who are you?"

Tim would respond almost impatiently, "Tim Murphy. Sir, you have a shiny bald head."

"Yes, that would be right," Jack Baker would say.

Things could go a number of ways at this point. Some people may have realized Tim was not like other kids and react either patronizingly or with hesitation. Most, though, to my relief, would continue along pleasantly, even when Tim would ask, "Can I pat your head?"

Oh, God, I'd think, *please say yes please be nice please* . . . and just then the man would lean over and present his head to Tim. Tim would then giggle and thank him and stroll ahead of me, with a kind of renewed sense of purpose, into the drugstore. He would mumble, "Jack Baker, shiny bald head [giggle]. Baker comma Jack, a balding man . . ."

Usually Tim liked to quiz us—his siblings—on who we knew with shiny bald heads. The list was short, always the same, yet the answers were always received by Tim with the enthusiasm of the first time.

"Ah, Cara?"

"Yes, Tim."

"Do you know anyone with a shiny bald head?"

"There's John [my godfather], Mr. Lang [a neighbor], Mr. Hanford with the putting green [another neighbor], Uncle Joe [our father's cigar-waving uncle]."

"What about Mr. Gold [Tim's psychologist], Cara?"

"Oh yeah, but I don't know him."

When I was a baby, Tim had a texture obsession for nylon stockings or pantyhose. This was very short lived, I think, because of the yelling and screaming that erupted when Tim, four, ran his hands down the stockinged legs of some supermarket shoppers.

But Mom would often fondly reminisce over this phase.

"Shopping with you, an infant, and keeping track of Tim was a nightmare," she told me. "It wasn't until I'd hear 'Shriek! Shriek!' and see streaks of women going past in opposite directions with their shopping carts that I knew Tim had to be nearby."

And for years Tim had an olfactory obsession with new shoes. It became routine for me to present Tim with the box holding my newly purchased shoes as soon as Mom and I walked through the door. He'd open the box, smell the shoes, and hand it back to me. I'd just watch him and then smell them myself, noting the smell of rubber mixed in with something else—was it cardboard, tissue paper, or just glue and chemicals? The smell *was* interesting. Some of my brother's pleasures did, in fact, make sense to me.

* * *

That February morning, while the snow continued to fall and the drifts continued to grow, I told Mom that I would check Tim's bedroom, since there was a chance he'd just stomped back to bed while I was outside. I started to feel sicker and sicker to my stomach as I grimly climbed the stairs to his bedroom, knowing he wouldn't be there. I stood in his room and wondered if Mom would call the police now. I looked out Tim's bedroom window at the snow falling, and I wished that our older brothers, both away at college, were home because I knew they would find Tim, somehow.

The outside house lights were still on, and through the curtain of snow, I could see Mom, right where I left her in the driveway, talking to Tim. I ran down the stairs; as I reached the front hall, I saw Tim pulling his boots off in the doorway.

"Ah, Cara, did you tell Mom that I haven't delivered my newspapers yet?" he asked, looking not at all as if he'd been wandering around for two hours in subzero temperatures.

"No, not that. I mean, yeah, I did all the papers a long time ago…but where have you been all morning?"

"I ran until I got too tired to run anymore," he said. "So, ah, Cara? You delivered all the papers on the Big Block, too?"

I realized that Tim felt as if he had done something wrong. It also occurred to me that he often focused less on what had been done to him and more on what he had done. I struggled to think of something I could say to him or give to him that would make

190

him feel happy. A hug wouldn't work; Tim did not like being hugged.

"I'm sorry that I made you mad," I said, since it was the only thing I could think to do.

"I forgive you, Cara. Cara, I'm going to take a shower now," Tim said, and headed upstairs.

By now Mom was making her coffee and looking at the newspaper on the kitchen counter. It seemed that she and Tim had talked about where he'd gone. After he stopped running, he went by his friend Van's house; and since Van's family was up early on Sundays for church, they asked Tim in, and he had a hearty Sunday breakfast with that family of six kids.

While Tim's return had a happy ending—and a happy middle, actually—I was getting used to the feeling of gratitude. As the youngest of four siblings, I had never had to take responsibility for anything. From that day on, I would try to remember to see the world through Tim's eyes. I would not forget that I needed to watch out for my big brother.

Sisters Aren't Doing It for Themselves

Negotiating Special Identities in a Disabled Family

Alison Wilde

Preamble

I was special. My brothers were special, too. Not as special as my sister, but definitely special and privileged in a way that few other people are. I was reassured by adults that Sarah, my sister, gave us gifts beyond measure. Why? Because, they said, she taught her siblings how to care. I tried to believe this back in the 1970s, in the northwest of England, because this was the only explanation we were given and the only way we could make sense of our situation. I don't believe it now.

I always wanted a sister. Living as the middle child in a male-dominated household, I yearned for sisterhood, for someone to share things with. Being eight years old, I was growing a little bored of my Tiny Tears doll and wanted a real baby to play with. The day of my sister's birth finally arrived; but, contrary to the joyous celebrations I had anticipated, a strange silence surrounded

Sarah when she was brought home, a silence of disappointment and grief that was never really broken. It was some time later before I knew the reasons for these emotions and began to question the woeful attitudes toward her life, something I would feel ashamed to divulge if she could understand the meanings of the words.

I would like to ask Sarah's permission to write this essay, as I have done with my brothers. This is something of an understatement—I would *love* to talk with my sister, something that will never happen. It is more than probable that she wishes the same so that she can communicate her choices, her wants, and desires. For many years I have had to guess how she feels and what she wants, as she cannot speak or make her thoughts known to anyone, having autism and "severe learning difficulties." Indeed, this predicament has also stimulated a lifelong interest in how we can respond with empathy to the needs of people who cannot communicate their needs and desires, even if disabling barriers were removed. In this instance, I feel a little ambivalent about writing about her, when she cannot know or respond to what I say. So, I'll be keeping my comments about Sarah to a minimum. In the following paragraphs, I will discuss myself, refer to my brothers' and parents' experiences[1] and stick to the issues of central concern: the disabling world we were plunged into after the birth of Sarah, my attempts to understand it, and the complexity of my psychoemotional responses to disability and concepts of care.

Being Sarah's sister: the early years

I began to question stigmatizing attitudes to disability and impairment after experiencing "courtesy stigma" at nine years of age as Sarah's sister. In public, I learned a great deal about attitudes toward disability and normality as Sarah was constantly subjected to insulting comments and looks or stares of horror, pity, and ridicule, gestures that were extended to other members of the family, sometimes in her absence.[2] In the more private realm of home life, I learned a lot about care and responsibility, lessons that took many years to unlearn.

From the day my sister was brought home from the hospital, my growing interest in the ways that meanings were imputed to impairment, disability, and care were stimulated by an ill-fitting or dissonant range of "situated knowledges" (Haraway 1991). These different and often contradictory ways of understanding disability were gained primarily from my previous interactions as a nondisabled child and avid reader of children's literature and these sudden new experiences. Perhaps most fundamentally, at nine years of age, my previous attitudes, based on a nondisabled positioning toward impairment and disability, shifted as I learned to occupy what felt like a liminal zone: the sister of a disabled person, neither disabled nor nondisabled.

My parents struggled for the first few years of her life to find answers to "what was wrong" with Sarah. By the time she received her diagnosis of "profound brain damage" around the age of five, we were more than aware that she "had problems." She couldn't walk, talk, or make communications that were meaningful, and she didn't seem to connect with anyone in nonverbal ways beyond very brief glances. The only thing we really knew was that she had epilepsy, as we had regularly assisted our parents with Sarah's grand mal fits, which usually started at 4:30 a.m. and often continued until 8 a.m.

Sadly, support given to the family was negligible; my parents were given no clear diagnosis or ideas of what the future would hold. Professionals seemed to avoid giving information or help, constantly deferring judgments on her health and her welfare and leaving the family effectively unsupported. In a way, then, it was understandable, given this vacuum and onerous responsibilities, that my parents turned to a "miracle cure" developed in the United States. They learned more about Sarah's multiple impairments from The Institutes for the Achievement of Human Potential (IAHP), an organization dedicated to using physical therapies and other learning strategies to increase brain development for "brain injured" and nondisabled children. My parents hoped they

195

could make Sarah "normal" or, at the very least, less "disabled" with the help of the IAHP's treatments.

Ironically, life eventually became somewhat stranger than the fiction I had been so fond of, as our home was transformed into a therapy center, aimed at effecting my sister Sarah's "cure." As Chrissie Rogers explains in *Parenting and Inclusive Education: Discovering Difference, Experiencing Difficulty* (2007), denials of the realities of having a disabled child are common, and the hope that the situation or impairment can be changed is often welcomed by parents, despite the evidence. I believe this was especially true in our case, as no professionals were explaining Sarah's impairments, no respite opportunities or other forms of support were given to the family, and, perhaps most importantly, nothing was offered to help us with the complex and intense range of emotions we experienced in trying to understand impairment, disability, and the so-called normality we had left behind. Fundamentally, we were learning to perceive the disabling world as an individual- and family-based pathology, as *our* problems that *we* had to fight for the good of us all.

Seeking the cure, killing the family

> Parents of brain-injured children are sometimes concerned about what will happen to their well children when they undertake The Institutes program. The answer is that they will benefit immensely. (IAHP 2010)[3]

Taking the path to normalization, my parents read an article in the local newspaper about remedial therapies that improved or overcame "brain injury." They raised money and enlisted Sarah in the IAHP. Under the approach developed by Glenn Doman and Carl Delacato,[4] the IAHP's programs were designed in Philadelphia, with only a small reassessment center in the United Kingdom (Midlands). The program the IAHP devised for Sarah demanded the involvement of the whole family and members of the community. We participated in a range of physically orientated tasks with her for an average of ten hours a day, some of which demanded a team of four volunteers. This was a grueling program, and there was a constant stream of sympathetic volunteers in our home. At the time, we felt brave and charitable, that our efforts were proof of our love and concern for her; but in attempting to "normalize" Sarah we were complicit with the devaluation of her life and the consequent "abnormalization" of our own lives. Most of her everyday life was spent in (strenuous) therapeutic activities, and the whole family was robbed of the (comparatively) private lives we had previously enjoyed. Living a "front-stage" private life also taught me how I should be performing as a girl, as a "carer."

As arduous as our lives were, dealing with Sarah's health and other needs, managing a constant stream of visitors and helpers in our home, and putting our own personal needs last, it was the social stigma and reduced social roles that were the hardest to endure. We were expected to work hard on the program and act as host to the volunteers who were ever-present in our home. I had already learned that such a visible impairment in the family had changed my expected roles as a female child and (less so, it felt) those of my brothers. My brothers continued a long tradition of family involvement in rugby and cricket, being accomplished sportsmen, whereas my passions were largely overtaken by everyday duties. I recall fear at attending school as I rarely got time to do homework and finished school with a poor set of results. It wasn't until I secured a university place, in my mid-twenties, that my disappointment in myself was felt as a deep and bitter resentment. This was initially felt as anger at what I perceived as my parents' neglect but was eventually focused on the social world, the professions and organizations that left us and continue to leave other disabled families misinformed, unsupported, and stranded.

The IAHP still insists that parents' participation in the program will "enhance significantly the development of their children physically, intellectually, and socially in a joyous and sensible way" (IAHP 2010).[5] In no way was this true for us. I was exhausted, intellectual pursuits were marginalized, and the pressures and responsibilities placed on me were senseless, dividing me from my peers, often making me miserable and anxious. And the constant message received from my parents, from professionals, and from the IAHP—that we were special, even privileged to be having these experiences—led to a redoubling of feelings of failure, as all I really wanted was my childhood back (as imperfect as it may have been).

Reflections

I had learned as a child that such a visible impairment in the family had changed my expected roles as a girl and that caring was an extremely gendered ideal. Overall, like many nondisabled people, I found that my previous understandings of disability had been largely misinformed by literature and other media representations. The frailty of female disabled characters and the "goodness" of their carers no longer held any appeal, as our experiences bore little or no resemblance to these portrayals, contributing to feelings of abnormality, isolation, and resentment. In terms of my identity, I felt myself to be a failure *as a girl*, while my mum seemed to have changed into little more than a caretaker. Later, I found that my own family's marked disparities in caring responsibilities were commonplace within other disabled families, curtailing other opportunities, particularly for women (Finch and Groves 1983).

My feelings toward Sarah have always been complex. As a child, I was burdened with feelings of guilt, sorrow, and humiliation. I had a growing sense of isolation coupled with a fear of the shame and anger arising at our stigmatized identities. I also learned much about charity. My father and his friends had set up a charity to raise the funds for my sister's program. Grateful for the kindness of others for donating gifts and money toward her cure, we were subjected to intense scrutiny as time went by. We were interrogated about everyday lives: how we'd found the money for a tape recorder, why Sarah wasn't improving, whether we were working hard enough and utilizing the funds properly, why one of us had been seen chatting or laughing outside the house. Consequently, I am filled with distrust about charity and the charitable impulse to the present day.

Later, having thrown heart and soul into this ill-conceived mission to improve or cure my sister's impairments, I was often filled with a sense of futility in embarking on long-term projects. I was, for example, all too aware that great efforts and sacrifice did not guarantee success and could easily lead to misery. The pressures on our family were unsustainable, and our parents ended their marriage when Sarah was seven, creating further hardship and considerable trauma. Within two years, my mother's lack of resources, financial, emotional, and social, led her to a decision to place Sarah in a large hospital for people with learning difficulties, a terrible decision for anyone to have to make.

In the same year, at the age of seventeen, I started work in a residential school for people with learning and behavioral difficulties. This job allowed me to turn my experiences to my advantage and offer some financial support to my mother, while escaping my family home for the first time. Four years later, I succeeded in gaining a place as a trainee nurse in the hospital where my sister lived, which meant I could see her nearly every day and check on her welfare. My fears about the treatment given to inmates of this hospital were confirmed. There was a widespread culture of institutional abuse which few, if any, of the "patients" escaped, regardless of impairment. The hospital was, I'm happy to say, closed as part of the deinstitutionalization process a few years later, and people were moved out to community care and smaller care units. Despite the fact that the torture of patients was an everyday, expected occurrence, I learned much about attitudes toward disabled people and their families from the hospital staff.[6] I was also horrified to find that there was little institutional desire to change the conditions of disabled lives, after reporting occurrences and the culture of abuse to a senior member of the health authority, who told me to "keep my mouth shut and my head down." He advised me that I would never be employed by them after qualification and that I would not be welcome in the hospital. While it was clear that there was little recognition of disabled people's lives as equally valuable (or worth anything at all, in many cases), the families of the residents were despised by most staff, for "dumping" their children or siblings in the hospital and seeking to live lives independent of them. I, of course, was one of them; I felt I had failed my sister—again.

Negotiating a special identity

> The belief in personal specialness is extraordinarily adaptive and permits us to emerge from nature and to tolerate the accompanying dysphoria: the isolation; the awareness of our smallness and the awesomeness of the external world, of our parents' inadequacies, of our creatureliness, of the bodily functions that tie us to nature; and, most of all, the knowledge of the death which rumbles unceasingly at the edge of unconsciousness. (Yalom 1980, p.121)

My mother's repeated insistence that I was special acted as a comfort and as a catalyst for resilience and pride in an otherwise harsh environment, as Irvin Yalom's ideas on specialness suggest. Our complaints that we didn't want to help with Sarah or distress at the ridicule and bullying from classmates were often met with explanations that we had more loving and empathetic personalities. In these circumstances, feeling special possibly helped me to face the vicissitudes of everyday life but also encouraged a disposition where my own identity was shaped primarily in terms of my function in helping others, resulting in (often simultaneous) feelings of worthlessness, emptiness, and superiority.

While I carried the "special" identity, I also carried the extra burdens of exclusion, disappointment, denial, and, most importantly, self-abnegation and overaccommodation.[7] Unfortunately, the process of reshaping my life has taken a long time, curtailing my opportunities as an adult. Nonetheless, my adult identity as a disabled person and mother of a son with Asperger syndrome gave me further opportunities to consider dismantling the yoke of specialness. When my academic interests carried me toward Disability Studies, these shackles began to break. Keen to refuse the special identities attributed to myself and my siblings, I endeavored to avoid discourses of exceptionality when bringing up my son. Like my parents, I now know that I only had a small, if crucial, part to play in this process, a drop of opposition in an ocean of disabling forces.

I will always feel privileged to have a sister like Sarah—she is as precious as my brothers, no more, no less. Ideally, I believe that siblings should live interdependently, contributing to the family and being nurtured by it. This should not make us special. Indeed, interdependence and mutual responsibility have much to contribute to mainstream culture, which promotes consumerist models of parenting and strategies of benign neglect as "normal" ways of doing family. Currently, we have done little to change things for disabled families and the siblings of disabled children, especially in the case of support for single parents. I fear that siblings of disabled children will continue to be labeled as victims, heroic, unfortunate, and long-suffering while an individualistic ethic toward disability prevails and social support is pathologized.

Notes

1. I am very grateful to my brothers Tim and Simon and my mother Cynthia for giving me permission to recount these experiences and to Tim and my mother for helping me fill in some of the gaps in my memory.

2. Since writing the first draft of this essay, I have spoken to my younger brother, Tim, about these experiences, but he recalls these situations in a very different way. He reminded me of a sense of pride in being her sibling. This was foremost in his memory, whereas I recall the sense of stigmatization and resentment toward public attitudes.

3. This claim is currently on IAHP's website: www.iahp.org. Arti.226+M54aa41872ca.0.html, accessed 27 Febuary 2010.

4. Glenn Doman is a physical therapist and Carl Delacato is an educational psychologist. They founded the IAHP and led the team who devised tailored programs for each child.

5. Also on the IAHP website: http://72.3.247.16/The-Institutes-for-the-Ach.7+M57ef1df55591.0.html?&tx_ttnews[pointer]=2, accessed 27 February 2010.

6. Routine actions from staff included sticking sellotape on the heads of people with autism, locking naked people in toilets and throwing buckets

of cold water over them, nurses pretending that they were going to set fire to an older resident (with autism) by stuffing her dress with paper and holding a lighter near her.

7. I am indebted to Mike Turton for helping me to recognize my tendency to overaccommodate other people's feelings and behaviors, enabling me to find the roots and consequences of this disposition. He also provided feedback that helped me feel parented, helping me to begin the process of self-parenting.

References

Finch, J. and Groves, D. (eds) (1983) *Labour of Love: Women Working and Caring.* London: Routledge and Kegan Paul.

Haraway, D.J. (1991) "Situated Knowledges: The Science Question in Feminism and the Privilege of Partial Perspective," in *Simians, Cyborgs and Women.* New York: Free Association Books.

Rogers, C. (2007) *Parenting and Inclusive Education: Discovering Difference, Experiencing Difficulty.* London: Palgrave Macmillan.

Yalom, I.D. (1980) *Existential Psychotherapy.* New York: Basic Books.

This Night Will Pass

15

Thomas Caramagno

Joe David is my younger brother and my shadow. We were born only eighteen months apart, 1946 and 1947, but he seemed remote, held captive in another universe, a strange and unreachable figure who was aloof yet fragile. I spent much of my childhood either running to or away from him. He perplexed and troubled me, yet I was drawn to him, like a puzzle you cannot solve but cannot put down. What was my kinship with this enigmatic phantom who squinted at me out of the corner of his eye, talked to himself in public, and seemed more enchanted than ill? Families today have resources to help them understand autism and provide the best practices for coping. We had less than nothing. It was a time of misinformation and misdiagnosis, of Freudian metaphors about empty fortresses and refrigerator mothers. Self-doubt sapped a family's strength and hope that an autistic child was a blessing, not a guilty secret to be hidden away in an institution. Many were sent away in those days.

This is a story about groping in the dark. I could not see my brother clearly or guess what he was thinking, what he was feeling. His mysterious anxieties seemed ridiculous to me, his sudden fears exaggerated. My father had grown up in Sicily, in poverty, and taught us the virtue of cold self-control, so Joe David's childish outbursts embarrassed me. Whatever moments of empathy slipped up on me unawares quickly turned to fear. Secretly, I hoped he could not really see me either or all the sharp, ungenerous feelings I hid from him and from everyone else. I was expected by my family to look out for him, and the photograph below, taken in 1955 by my mother, suggests I did my duty, though I have wondered all my life if my heart was really in it.

There we are, looking as if we were chums. I am holding him in place for the camera, posing him, perhaps against his will, as if for the appearance of normalcy. I helped my mother take care of him. He and I shared a bedroom, I tried to teach him how to play, I protected him from other children, and once tried to fight off two field rats that sent us both to the emergency room. Was I good to him? I tried to be. But I can't remember. It's difficult to recall positive events, those sepia-toned memories you can chat about fifty years later at family gatherings with a wistful fondness. My past fits me like a hair shirt. In reading my mother's diary to prepare for writing this essay, I found her remembrance that I spoke kindly to Joe David. She said she was grateful for that. But I can't remember whether I did or not. I am nagged by doubts that color the past, not sepia, just dark. How much of my helpfulness was merely an attempt to please her or to uphold my image as protector or to hide my disappointment that he would never be the brother I had always wanted? I watched movies on television, *Beau Geste, Gunga Din, Robin Hood*, with swashbuckling brothers-in-arms, dreaming what it could have been like had our family been "normal." When the Kennedy brothers played touch football on the White House lawn, I daydreamed that we could have been them.

There was a lot of make-believe in those days. Nobody imposed it. Or had to. We were all conspirators, maintaining the image of a modern family that understood Joe David's condition, that was "dealing with it" in a thoroughly modern way, with no collateral damage. But there was damage. I felt as if I had lost a brother, and I did not know what to do with this loss. I could not grieve openly, not for him, not for myself, for he was still needful of care, locked away in some terrible, dark abyss that was his eyes.

For me, Joe David's eyes lie at the center of it all. The child psychologist D. W. Winnicott theorized that good mothering begins with benevolent eye contact, that intimate, playful give-and-take when infant and mother look fondly on one another, reading themselves and their worth in what they see in the eyes of the other. This primal pairing becomes the model for other relationships; even if we reject, amend, or improve on it, it is always there. I think this applies to siblings as well. Their regard stamps us indelibly with a seal of approval, a value that confers confidence we can repay all debts of family, friendship, and love. But Joe David could not give me what I wanted. He could not even look at me. Here is a picture of him from 1963: his face is impenetrably blank. He is not really looking at the camera but at something else, something inside that held him enthralled in a trance I could not break.

Like a cat, he felt compelled to turn away from me, threatened by my gaze, denying me his. And in that denial, I took childish offense. I couldn't understand what obstacle was coming between us, so I blamed him for it and then blamed myself. I resented the attention he received from others without earning it. I felt guilty when I withheld what I could have offered him, *should* have offered, a brother's pledge that he would be safe in something larger than himself, even if he could not partake in family life the way the rest of us could.

My adult life replayed this underlying theme, trying to earn recognition, even love, through overachievement, hyperalert to minute alterations in the attention of others, fearful that I was losing their affection, with no hope of crossing that gulf between my eyes and theirs. It was unconditional love that I craved, anxiety's respite, a soft, benevolent flood into all the corners of the soul, deeper than thought or duty or disability. Did Joe David feel it? I could never tell. He never showed it. Was he incapable or just unwilling? To a child's mind, these two terms are hard to keep separate. Whenever I asked him how he was feeling, he would say, "I don't know," and I could interpret that in two ways: he did not *know* how to put his feelings into words; he did not *want* to say, at least to me.

It is a paradox of human nature, but ubiquitous, that when you cannot accept others' limitations, you cannot accept your own. I campaigned for acceptance, pined for recognition, in academia worked myself nearly to death for fellowships, grants, appointments. I survived cancer, heart surgery, even tenure. You know the old saying that professors must "publish or perish." I was managing to do both. I could earn tenure but not a gift like love. It is either given or withheld, and no effort, however herculean, can win it back once it is lost. I am sixty-four years old now. I've done all the proving I can do. It is time to look back and sum up my life, find either integrity or despair, and finish the job. T. S. Eliot said it best in "East Coker": "In my beginning is my end."

My beginning lies somewhere buried in the ancient maze of conflicted feelings that is my childhood, at the center of which is, and always has been, my autistic brother. When Deb Cumberland asked me to contribute an essay to this book on siblings of autistic children, I grabbed at the chance to recap, and perhaps redeem, the past. Our life stories must be told and retold before all their meanings can be grasped. After her death, my mother left me with boxes of old, handwritten notebooks; black-and-white photographs; rejected applications to programs for the disabled; medical records from doctors, neurologists, psychiatrists, and social workers; a mountain of bureaucracy she had climbed without complaint for Joe David's sake. I went through it hoping to find that sake.

Joe David was born on August 17, 1947, at Queen of Angels Hospital on Alvarado Street near downtown Los Angeles, the same hospital I was born in. He was a healthy child from the start. But he was different. Look at this photo:

He always had that worried look in his face. Daily life for him was chaotic and unpredictable. Like many autistic children, he went through a terrible period of shattering tantrums and troubled sleep from about two-and-a-half to six years of age. He bit people and was very unhappy, though we could never figure out what was making him unhappy and he could never tell us. There were victories too, which I did not know about until I read my mother's notes. As an infant, he was terrorized by buzzing noises: vacuums, electric clippers, radio static. My mother employed desensitization methods to accustom him gradually to irritant noises, comforting him at each stage of increasing volume. It not only worked but eventually changed aversion to fascination, and in his adolescence, he began tape recording any errant sounds he came across. Technology helped him vanquish his fear of the unexpected. He could study it, identify its patterns, and categorize what at first seemed only amorphous and frightening. One evening at the dinner table, he announced that he could identify any diverse sound produced by electrical transmissions, and this triumph was deeply satisfying to him. Thereafter, he became a dynamo of activity and invention. Everywhere he went, he was weighed down like a soldier with backpacks full of electronic gadgets, some of his own making, whose purpose and utility were mysteries to us. But they meant something important to him. They helped him translate the world.

Joe David had all the classic signs of autism, but no one recognized them for what they were at the time. When my mother held him, he hung limply in her arms, like a ragdoll. He never asked to be picked up, nor did he notice whether she was in the room or not. In her notebooks, which she had started in 1950 to chronicle his development, she wrote that Joe David never established eye contact with her, except once, when he was five months old, when he "suddenly turned his head around and looked searchingly into my eyes for perhaps 15 seconds. Otherwise, he never noticed or cared who was taking care of him. I tried and tried to get him to look at me and failed." She took it hard, blaming herself. She had *failed*, and that responsibility demanded a lifetime of reparation. Even when she was dying, in her eighty-sixth year, she told me that she still felt guilty about Joe David, though by that time she knew that autism was not psychogenic and could not have been her fault. But old tapes kept playing.

When not placidly indifferent, Joe David was easily frustrated, which triggered great anxiety, hand-flapping, striking his head with his hand or a wall. My mother would sweep him up into her arms and try to calm him down. Sometimes he reacted with complete withdrawal: he would sit alone, rocking in a chair and staring off into the distance. We didn't know what to do then. What was he seeing that I couldn't? I wondered. The Catholic priests at my church talked of beatific visions and holy raptures transporting the saints and martyrs at the time of greatest peril. Murals depicted these trances when pagans and infidels filled their bodies with spears. I would stare at them for hours, looking for some resemblance to Joe David's trances. But he seemed neither rapturous nor transported. Just absent.

There were other signs we were slow to interpret because we didn't understand what autism was. When he crawled on the floor, it was always along the lines of a wall, a fence, or a sidewalk, as if he needed guidance in the wild world. Inconsistencies in food brought him to an abrupt halt: he adamantly refused to eat fruits, vegetables, or chopped food. Even today, at age sixty-two, his diet consists mainly of fast food, pasta, and cookies. At the time, I thought it was just obstinacy, but there was something about the texture of certain foods that repulsed him, not the flavor. It was twenty-five years later before a psychologist explained to us that Joe David's perception of the world was so erratic yet so intense that he must have been struggling to find any stability. We all depend on food to be predictable. That first taste of a meal is really a leap into the unknown. Sight, smell, texture, taste—all must justify the risk of trespassing the border between outside and inside. If food can shift, waver, or morph without warning, how can anyone feel safe? And when the Self also wavers, what then?

It's all about perception. It was not our fault, the psychologist said reassuringly, that Joe David lived in an intemperate world; but we had become so habituated to guilt that we never really let it go, especially my mother.

Getting professional help for my brother in those days was extremely difficult. Younger readers must remember that early infantile autism was not even recognized until 1943 when Leo Kanner distinguished it from schizophrenia. Most psychologists in the 1950s believed that as many as ninety percent of autistics were destined to live out their lives in institutions. Few parents were able to care for them at home, for there were no guidelines and no reassurances that improvements were possible. My mother was constantly knocking on doors to find anyone who could help or even assign a proper diagnosis. Joe David received many of those, everything from childhood schizophrenia or severe brain damage to manic-depression, cerebral palsy, or mental retardation. In her notebook, my mother once wrote in exasperation: "Most autistic children have collected a variety of diagnoses. The strangest one I've heard is 'pseudo-psychotic psychosis,' which apparently means a psychosis that imitates a psychosis." How can a psychosis imitate a psychosis? We didn't know. Which was the real psychosis? Did it even matter? We didn't know that either. She had studied nursing in college in the late 1930s, not psychology, but being Joe David's mother required that she educate herself in a subject that was, at the time, on the verge of undergoing a massive reevaluation. Bruno Bettelheim's hypothesis that autism was the result of poor parenting, particularly "refrigerator mothers" who were cold, rejecting, and intellectual, added to her guilt. Intelligent women were routinely ridiculed as unfeminine in those days, and blaming mothers for a child's condition was at its height of popularity in psychoanalytic corners. My mother was never cold or rejecting, but she was definitely an intellectual, which complicated things, especially in a family line weighted genetically for depression over several generations. Bettelheim just made it worse.

But even while she bore the burden of guilt, my mother harbored another impulse that counterbalanced the negative with a healthy skepticism and a lifelong desire to learn. She joined other parents in what became a decades-long fight to redeem the families of autistics. In 1965, she, other parents of autistic children, and Dr. Bernard Rimland, a pioneer in developing the diagnostic criteria for autism, established the Southern California Autistic Society, which has become a preeminent site for information sharing and support. She worked unpaid for that group for twenty-five years, publishing summaries of papers and studies presented at conferences. She participated in genetic studies at UCLA. And in her fifties, she went back to school, earning a double B.S. in biology and psychology. In spite of all this effort and success, in the end my mother still felt she should have done more. Intellectually, she knew that Joe David's condition was not her fault. But, emotionally, the old tapes played an old song that depression reinforced: "You're not good enough. There's something wrong with you." And Joe David became the proof of that.

* * *

The 1950s was a decade of fruitless search for my mother. The Spastic Children's Foundation allowed Joe David to enroll for one year only because they judged him "physically retarded"— he couldn't climb stairs—but he was also socially withdrawn and not able to participate in structured group activity. The foundation's pediatrician was sharp enough to write in his clinical notes that Joe David "does not seem to recognize people as individuals nor to respond to one voice more than another." He did not even recognize himself in a mirror, so after a year he was dis-enrolled. My mother took him to other groups in the Los Angeles area—the Exceptional Children's Foundation, Fairview State Hospital, the PAR Workshop, the Parents Training Center, the Moore-White Medical Clinic, and the State Department of

Rehabilitation—each saw its own diagnostic bias in Joe David, and so he was passed from one agency to the another until, finally, a child psychiatrist at UCLA's Neuropsychiatric Institute, James Q. Simmons, diagnosed him correctly as autistic in 1978. By that time, Joe David was already thirty-one years old.

Meanwhile, though inept socially, Joe David increasingly mastered mechanical skills: the occupational therapist at the Spastic Children's Foundation taught him how to pour sawdust from one container to another, and he brought this skill home, where he poured cups of water in the bathtub. When the outpatient program was shut down, my mother and other parents started their own school, which operated from 1951 to 1959. Instead of forbidding self-stimulation, as was the custom then, they tried to keep the children busy with other rewarding activities. In her diary, my mother wrote: "We had warm and cold pools, mud pools, finger paints, balloons that we popped, music, materials of all kinds of textures. We had swings, a tunnel and a jumping bed, and a slide." I have a dozen notebooks with such observations written down by various parents about how each child responded and progressed. Unfortunately, the parents were also spending a great deal of time psychoanalyzing themselves because the Bettelheim approach was so prevalent. I remember going to various clinicians who were also under the impression that only a neurotic family could produce an autistic child, and we usually left feeling depressed. No matter how hard we searched ourselves for unconscious motives that must have injured Joe David, we found either nothing or too many things. It was easy to privilege even the most common impulse or event as causative because we were desperate to find something. And the psychoanalytic technique of reading everything as a symptom had no brakes. We were three brothers, Joe David the youngest; did that have something to do with it? My father had only a grade-school education; my mother was well read. Did that trap Joe David into an Oedipal conflict? There were so many paths we could follow. One memory in particular stands out. It was the summer of 1963, and we were in family therapy at the Kennedy Child Study Center when the psychologist suddenly began talking about me in the third person, even though I was sitting there not three feet from him. Addressing only my parents, he discussed the probability that I was shutting myself off emotionally and would likely suffer the consequences of it for years to come. I felt suddenly transparent, as if I were a "case," not a person. I didn't rock or flap my hands, but my impression was that I might, just might, become Joe David, if I didn't watch out. After all, I too felt uneasy whenever I looked at myself in a mirror, as if one day I might see only a stranger where I was supposed to be.

It was as if a spell had been cast over me, so I tried to escape. I moved to on-campus quarters when I began college, and while I let my studies slide, I immersed myself in acting for Loyola Marymount's Del Rey Players. If I found my own skin unreal and unlovable, I could at least become someone else for two hours a performance, four nights a week. I auditioned for every role that came my way. While tragedies gave me the creeps, I excelled at comedic parts, pretending joy. I had already rehearsed that role very well. I received quotable reviews in the local newspaper as Ensign Pulver in *Mr. Roberts*. I "killed" as Snoopy in *You're A Good Man, Charlie Brown*. I was dancing as fast I could, trying to deny the obvious: that I didn't know who I was. All I knew was that what I could do, Joe David couldn't. But self-esteem came at a price. Any inadvertent remark that questioned my competence was met by a surge of anxiety and defensive anger. I argued without mercy points that weren't worth arguing in the first place. I pushed people away from me before they discovered just how misplaced their affection was. I fell in love with a brilliant young woman who later became a psychiatrist specializing in autism. Odd, how all these convergences happen, isn't it? Or is it Joe David again? Always the center knot in my tangled life? When she broke up with me because I had no similar academic ambitions, in despair I pounced on a new identity: I would become an intellectual superstar and win her back. I had read *The Great Gatsby*. I would get a PhD too and teach and write books —proving, once and for all, that I would not become my brother.

And I succeeded, in a way. Even pseudo-identities can succeed "in a way," but always in a very defective way. I earned my doctorate in English from UCLA and three MA's, the last, in clinical psychology, in my late fifties. Like my mother, I was the oldest in my class. I did all that was required. I earned tenure. Twice. I published scholarly books, one on Virginia Woolf and manic-depression that challenged the way psychoanalytically inclined critics infantilized her and blamed her parents for her condition. Notice the parallels? I did. I even won prizes, a year's fellowship at Harvard, a Fulbright in Lisbon; but I never felt that I had succeeded in proving the most important thing: that I was not Joe David. Eventually, and not surprisingly, I crashed and burned.

Ironically, even as I and my family were struggling with disappointment and guilt, Joe David himself made steady progress. It's true that he did not start to talk until age four and that he produced only nouns at first (and reversed pronouns, saying "you" for "me" and confusing "up" and "down," "on" and" under," etc.), like many other autistics, but by nine, he was speaking in whole paragraphs. He toilet-trained himself when he was five and had his first really good Christmas when he played with the toys instead of the wrappings. At seven years, he began to understand time and clocks. At nine, he could be trusted to go to the store alone, and that is when he learned to read and write. Both activities enhanced his ability to control himself. Given a book or a writing pad, he could sit quietly in public for an hour or more. His learning skills seemed to take off: he taught himself to ride a bike, fly a kite, and read a map. By the time he was in his mid-twenties, Joe David's vocabulary was equal to a college graduate's because, once he learned a word, he never forgot it.

He was, it turns out, a complicated creature, and resembled me in more ways than I cared to admit. Like other autistics, Joe David lacked gracefulness, standing at attention, rigid, stock still, even in casual situations. Here he is in the early 1970s:

Notice the shirt pocket full of pens (a habit I still have, too). Neither of us knew how to dress stylishly. Both of us wore corduroy pants and Hush Puppies long past the fashionable expiration date. And there are still times when I find myself standing at attention as he does, my arms thrust straight down, my hands fisted, pushed forward, as if I am restraining myself—or am I stiffening myself in anticipation of some assault? For Joe David, perception was assaultive or at least mysteriously inconstant: on vacations we would point out something of interest, and, if he couldn't see it, he would conclude, "Ah, it must be a ghost." I don't think he meant this literally; it was his way of admitting difficulty without getting upset about it. I too feel keenly frustrated, and embarrassed, when I misjudge reality, and I have certainly used rationalizations to explain it away. Joe David spent hours in his bedroom reciting aloud dialogue from the cartoon shows *The Flintstones*, *The Jetsons*, and *Yogi Bear*. I would entertain myself (and reluctant friends) reciting aloud dialog from *Road to Morocco*, *A Hard Day's Night*, and *Monty Python's Flying Circus*. He produced his own cartoons, filling his room with paper tablets colored with crayon, telling stories about the women he knew. I wrote a novel, telling stories about the women I knew and how mystifying relationships were to me. There was one significant difference between us: his stories were joyful, while mine were not. I remember hearing him laughing out loud in his room while composing a storyline. I never laughed.

Other traits were characteristically autistic. Joe David understood verbal statements more literally; he could not interpret proverbs, and irony escaped him. He talked either too loud or too soft. He would start a sentence several times before he could finish it. He was very bright in science but very naïve in social situations. His understanding of social customs was black or white. There were no nuanced, gray areas. We had to tell him, in absolutist terms, not to point to the bellies of pregnant women and ask, in a loud, unselfconscious voice, "Pardon me, but are you pregnant or just fat?" But, at the same time, he was quite aware that he was autistic and understood that it limited him. To his credit, he was willing to make what adjustments he could. He developed a strong sense of humor in adulthood, a ravenous appetite for puns, and he accumulated quite an encyclopedic knowledge of cartoons. His memory is still extraordinarily precise. Recently, I asked him, "Joe, do you remember when Papa took us to Huntington Lake? When was that? In the fifties or the sixties?" And he replied, "It was on October 11, 1958. That was the same day they launched Pioneer 1 toward the moon from Cape Canaveral. It weighed only eighty-three pounds." I once asked, "What's the area code for Cincinnati?" And he knew it. For extras, he added the zip code. He didn't do it to show off, as I would have. He did it because I might need to know. Knowledge is important to him. It makes the world go round. And he is completely dedicated to keeping the machine in working order.

How did all this progress happen? Although we were late to realize it, Joe David's talents had been evident from early on. My mother recorded in her diary that, once Joe David started to read, he became fascinated with books on electronics. He could define technical terms as if he had a photographic memory. He performed what my mother called "scientific experiments." One in particular stands out in my memory. On vacations, my father loved to drive up to Yosemite, Huntington Lake, or Puget Sound. Joe David noticed that insects would get caught in the honeycombed columns of the car's radiator. Each time we stopped, he got out and inspected them. When I asked him what he was looking for, he only said, "Melds." I didn't realize until much later that he was conducting basic research in an area defined by autism. He had noticed that insect bodies changed, warped by high temperatures. From his point of view, they started as one thing but became another thing. What more natural a subject of interest for someone who daily grapples with perceptual inconsistencies? His experiments with electronic circuits followed the same course. For instance, he recognized that there were different color temperatures in light, so he experimented with electronic circuitry until he found a way to measure them. As a teenager, he had learned to shop for electronic components and solder them together inside metal boxes. Strange, inexplicable designs. But they worked. Even now, whenever I drive him around town, he still points one of his instruments at street lamps or billboards or signal lights and tells me whether they are lit by filament, fluorescence, LED, or vaporized mercury. He announces this as if I needed the information, as if I also recognized that it was important to know my surroundings. He remembers the locations of each type of light, as if he is surveying the lay of the land, mapping out routes to orient himself when away from home, like Hansel and Gretel leaving bread crumbs.

When I was younger, it didn't occur to me that his technical wizardry might have been significant in another way, that while he was creating these devices, some of which seemed only to blink lights and do nothing else I could detect, I was building ham radios and shortwave receivers. Was this only a coincidence? Or a gesture at brotherhood? I shared my interest in electronics with my mother, who earned her own amateur radio license in 1965, but I didn't see Joe David's odd experiments as anything we could share. When I asked him how a device worked, he couldn't explain it in terms I could understand, so I dismissed it as an eccentricity. Is that the way he felt about my hobbies? Did building transmitters and receivers just to talk to strangers thousands of miles away strike him as a bootless waste of time? A few years ago I tried to introduce him to computers, thinking it would be a perfect match for his amazing grasp of details and order. Although he listened to my explanation with feigned interest, he was only humoring me and ignored the subject subsequently. I was stumped. His likes and dislikes never followed a logical course but were instead highly specific, based on particulars understandable only in his world.

A dramatic turning point in Joe David's development came in 1978 when, with the support of the Neuropsychiatric Institute's Dr. Simmons, he was moved to Santa Barbara to become part of an innovative program operated by the Tri-Counties Regional Center's Work-Training Program. Under their supervision, he lived in his own subsidized apartment, held a full-time job in a supervised sheltered workshop, and was routinely inspected by the supportive services coordinator, Carol Press. Carol was a godsend, a truly caring and organized person who made sure Joe David paid his bills on time, cleaned his apartment, and grew socially. When a girlfriend exploited him for money, Carol intervened. When another girlfriend stalked him, Carol obtained a restraining order. Although his susceptibility to being taken advantage of alarmed us, it also made us realize just how sympathetic Joe David could be. He gave the money to people because he felt sorry for them. It was a matter of social justice: he had money, and they did not. More than once he gave away money he was supposed to use for purchasing food. Two years ago, when he arrived at my house after a long train ride without having eaten at all that day, I asked him why he had done it: "She needed the money," he said. I talked about economic practicalities but suddenly remembered how my father spent his adult life working in the Teamsters Union for fair wages and how my mother sent monthly donations to Catholic charities: Mother Cabrini's orphanage and the Little Sisters of the Sacred Heart. Joe David was, in his own way, carrying on my parents' liberal tradition. Yes, his condition left him vulnerable to manipulation, but he also had sympathy for others, something we were told early on not to expect from an autistic.

His years in the Work Training Program (WTP) produced changes that constantly surprised and pleased us. When he first arrived there, he was still enclosed in the bell jar of autism. He talked to himself in public and tramped around town alone, laden with electric clocks, a neon lamp with a battery mounted on a soap dish, an underwater camera, a portable television set, and a "vibration detector" in a spice jar that was supposed to detect earthquakes. At first, he made no friends there, preferring to go home after work and sit at his desk where he performed his experiments. But, as time went by, Carol recorded continual progress. With each visit, we saw how much he had changed. We were, for instance, surprised to learn that he participated in the Special Olympics swimming events, had in fact trained for it at a local public pool, and eventually won four medals. He began attending the WTP Supportive Services graduate group, swimming with friends at the Diver's Den, and "hanging out" with another WTP member, Charleen, a twosome that Carol described as "a mutually satisfying relationship." His performance at work was applauded for its accuracy: not surprisingly, Joe worked in an electronic assembly room crimping Tilton wires, stripping staple wires, and racking oilwell Kilovac wires. This was child's play for him. He was taking the skills he had learned at home and applying them at work. But that was just a job. Although his bosses repeatedly offered him advancement, Joe always turned them down. It was the creative work at home he truly loved. Like Einstein in the patent office, Joe David was often caught daydreaming, but out of those dreamy speculations came inventions that pleased his curiosity about how things worked. It didn't matter that other people couldn't understand his pleasure. It didn't matter that it made no money. This I understood. My work, published in scholarly journals, made no money either. But it was important to me, making sense of the world, a way to step out of the bell jar of my own mind.

Look at this picture. It is amazing to me. There is genuine joy in his face. It was his birthday, and we had given him a Kodak Instamatic. We normally expected him to focus immediately on the gift, gluing his attention on it. But here he is more concerned with giving us a rewarding smile, holding up the gift and the birthday card for the occasion of a family photo. I wasn't posing him. He knew how to pose himself. His eyes were looking directly at us. At me, since I was holding the camera. We were all astonished. But now, as I look at this image, I am suddenly reminded of my father, after whom he was named. I had, for a long time, sympathized with my father for the bad luck of having the only son who was abnormal being named after him, the only son who really looked like him, with the same coal-dark eyes and black, curly Sicilian hair. Today I find comfort in looking at my brother because my parents are both dead, the past is gone, irretrievable, but I can see now that Joe David is their living legacy, doing things they did not dare hope for. Working at a job, living on his own, yet being part of a community has utterly transformed him. He has a full life, friends, hobbies, happiness. He has even joined a travel group for the disabled called New Directions; with them Joe David has hiked up the coastal mountains and visited Hawaii twice. He takes the train up from Santa Barbara to Folsom on holidays to visit us. And when he arrives, he does something outstanding, something my parents would have never expected. He asks me, "How are you?" He is beginning to talk about feelings, not just his, but other people's.

Joe David has blossomed. As I write this essay and look back over the years, I realize he had been slowly blossoming all along. It was I who underestimated him, and myself, for the capacity to find solace in simply being oneself. I am reminded of John Milton, who wrote in *Paradise Lost*: "The mind is its own place and in itself, can make a Heaven of Hell, a Hell of Heaven." Joe has made a Heaven. And I?

In my end is my beginning.

Sirens

16

Debra Cumberland

My mother was bombed twice, but I knew of none of it, until we went to Germany as a family for the first time. I was seven and in the first grade that hot, humid summer in 1973; I thought of Germany as a romantic, far-off place, a lot like Disneyland, a place where my mother said she was born and the place from which Uncle Karl and Aunt Ursula, Uncle Wolfgang and Aunt Regina sent brilliantly wrapped packages for every birthday and Christmas. But my mother never spoke of it romantically, if at all. She didn't speak in German—except occasionally to swear—and she rarely, if ever, spoke of wanting to go back.

I thought of Germany during the last muggy days of school, while I sat in front of the television, licking frosting off Oreo cookies and watching *Gilligan's Island*, *Bewitched*, or *Scooby Doo*. I was only dimly aware that the Vietnam War was coming to an end and that the U.S. was preparing to withdraw troops, although the bombing and the fighting would continue for sometime. But my mother made me aware that something was very, very wrong. She would stare at the television screen, her face taut with worry, and I would look at her, and lean a little closer to where she sat on the couch, and she would stroke my hair distractedly.

When we walked to the lake or went out for ice cream and saw planes fly overhead, she put her arm around me, and I could feel her body tremble slightly. She shook her head, and sighed, staring after the distant spiral curls from the plane, curls that arced upward, like hands outstretched, breaking the surface of the water. I knew that the sigh was not for the plane and not for the passengers, but for something deeper, something darker, something lying still and buried, under the surface of the water, waiting for me to find it. But I was timid in the face of my mother's distress and said nothing, just held her hand and waited for the light to change so we could cross the street. Neither one of us said anything.

* * *

All my father's students were talking. They came over to our house on the last day of my father's history class—U.S. foreign policy—and sat around the table, grabbing my mother's homemade oatmeal bread and slurping soup. I stared at them with my big eyes, their bell-bottom jeans, their long stringy hair. I heard words like "Nixon" and "fascist" and "pigs" and committed them to memory, determined to find out what they meant after dinner. One girl compared Nixon to a "Nazi," another word I had often heard but couldn't get an explanation for. When I finished dinner, I headed up the stairs to the living room to watch cartoons, only to see that once again *Gilligan's Island* wasn't on because of Nixon. "Pig," I said, relishing my new, fragrant vocabulary.

But none of it affected my older brother. He sat and rocked, sat and rocked, there on the living room floor, rocked and twirled pens; sometimes, he banged his head against the kitchen wall. I often felt that I should not bring friends over when my brother was acting like that, so I eventually quit asking. I rarely brought anyone home but broke away silently from the huddle of girls on the playground in their Brownie uniforms and Holly Hobby skirts and headed home quickly, afraid that someone might ask. I had the feeling that Adam might be a source of shame, a secret, much as my mother's past might be, although everyone knew she was German, knew she was from overseas. Someone had once drawn a swastika on her purse at a faculty event. My mother threw it out. She said nothing, just bit her lip, and told me what it was but not what it meant. She did not talk much of the past, so I did not ask, worried that I would cause that anxious look to come over her face.

"He can't help it, honey," my mother had told me, once when she was kneading bread, when my brother had nearly broken my father's hand by smashing his head against it, repeatedly, when my father placed his hand against the wall to prevent Adam from cracking his skull. "He has an illness, and it makes him do those things. But he is your brother, and you need to love him." I tried to take it all in, but it just made me feel small and frightened, the head-pounding, the talk of war, the students protesting, my mother's trembling hands as she passed me the communion tray at church. She could not control the trembling. And when the Sunday communion wine splashed across her dress, I pretended not to notice, sure her cheeks would be scarlet with embarrassment. My brother twirled his pen and rocked in the pew. I could hear my classmates giggling behind me. I tried to look cool, swinging my legs, coloring in my bulletin, while my mother frantically dabbed at the wine on her pale-yellow linen dress with a tissue and my brother twirled his pen. Soon we would be in Germany, I told myself, far away from all this. No one would know us in Germany, and if my autistic brother sat and rocked, no one here would know. It was hard to go anywhere with Adam. When we went to church potluck dinners, I stood in line, Adam behind me, conscious of the stares, the whispered comments. Once he ate twenty pieces of fried chicken and threw up, and after that, my mother said she could not go to any more church potlucks. I was sitting on the floor, playing Scrabble, when Phyllis Remington, the church busybody, called.

My mother, mustering all her courage, said no, we could not go, and hung up the phone, sighing. I didn't say anything. I knew there was no point. At that time, people didn't understand autism.

And there is still much confusion today. Psychologists such as Bruno Bettelheim, the infamous Viennese psychoanalysist, blamed it on the mother, as did Leo Kanner, an Austrian psychiatrist. Mothers who could not love their children, said Kanner, produced children who could not love. Bettelheim linked the autistic child with victims of torture and compared them to concentration camp victims. My mother knew these theories. She was told them by the doctors we saw. I've always wondered, now in hindsight, what my mother thought when she looked in her beautiful baby boy's distant and expressionless face. Did she hear those theories echo in her mind? Was she reminded of the war, again and again, a constant, relentless bombing, in the face of her anguished love?

* * *

Uncle Hans and Uncle Wolfgang picked us up at the airport in their Mercedes-Benz. Both were burly, slow-paced, bear-like men with soft, fleshy bodies. "I thought you would be fat," Wolfgang said, as he enveloped my mother in a hug. "You know our mother was pretty big when she was your age." He picked me up and twirled me, and I shrieked with delight. My mother did not look too happy and looked less happy when Wolfgang started barreling down the Autobahn at one hundred miles an hour. But Adam was ecstatic. He sat behind Wolfgang and counted the odometer miles, shrieking, one hundred, one hundred, over and over, until Wolfgang asked if we ever disciplined the boy.

We stayed in the house my mother grew up in, a two-story stucco with gooseberry bushes in the front and a cherry tree in the backyard. The summer was not as hot and the air was not as humid as it was back home. Here we did not have the storms my mother had grown to fear in Iowa, storms that sent her to the basement while my father stood out on the edge of the driveway, watching the thunderheads approach. "A tornado took all my hair, Debra," he told me once, and I stared at him quizzically, not sure whether to laugh. We spent many mornings in the Bergenswald; there, walking on the lush grass, underneath the shade of the chestnut trees, I heard stories about my mother (the mother who hid in the basement, the mother who did not like company) that made me stare at her in surprise: did I know that my mother had once outrun the French army? "Oh, don't tell her that," my mother protested, but it was true, my father said. He told me how, when she was barely in her teens, she was sent to visit her uncle in the Black Forest. The area was under French occupation, and they had very stringent rules for Germans since the spirit of revenge was strong. To get to her uncle's place, she had to pass the French army barracks. No German was permitted to walk on the sidewalk by the barracks. "Your mother thought it was ridiculous," continued my father, "and you know what she does when she thinks something's ridiculous." I nodded. "Well," continued my father, "she decided to violate the rule and walk on the sidewalk by the barracks. Her cousin, who was with her at the time, screamed at her to 'obey the rules.' When he saw she had no intention of walking on the street, he raced for his father's home, leaving her alone. Undaunted, your mother, pigtails waving in the breeze, walked brazenly down the sidewalk in defiance of the dictum of the French army. She was quickly spotted, and the entire troop came charging out of the barracks. So she ran. When she arrived at her uncle's home, the news had already spread. Her uncle phoned her grandfather, saying, 'Get her out of here—I am sending her back.'" I heard the slapping of boots on cement, imagined my mother racing ahead, looking behind and picking up the pace. Did I know that? No. And my mother could imitate the cuckoo bird. Really? My mother smiled, a slow, mysterious smile, and folded her slender hands together, cupped them against her mouth, and softly blew; Adam rubbed his nose with delight and tried, and soon the woods were echoing with cuckoo birds, until we all begged him to stop.

Visitors came several times a day, usually bringing candy, so I made sure to be near the door. I loved to hear the doorbell chime. The visitors would sit in the parlor, in pantsuits, in skirts and jackets, sometimes bringing flowers, and I would catch familiar phrases: usually Hans Erich, Hans Erich. One morning, after they left, I asked my mother, "Do they mean Uncle Hans?" And she shook her head, explaining that there was another Uncle Hans, and I remembered the picture back home, the one of a young man, with a sad, earnest face, his eyes gazing far away, a dark stain in the corner that my mother later explained was his blood. "He had the picture in his pocket when he died," my mother said, as we walked back into the living room, past the grandfather clock, past a gilded mirror, hanging in the hallway. "He had been killed in Russia." And she paused. We were standing in the entrance to the hallway, and she turned and gazed behind her, as if he might be there. "I was standing right here when I heard the news," she whispered. And she told me how, that night, her mother had rushed into the hallway. The mirror had shattered. The grandfather clock that she wound every night had stopped. And her mother had cried out, "Hans is dead, Hans is dead." He had lain in a Russian hospital, shot in the back. He had lain there for hours, not speaking. And my mother thought she knew why. He had lain there, longing to be with them, longing to tell them that he had been shot, that he was dying. And so he did not speak. He directed all his mental energy to communicate in another way: he had stopped the clock. He had shattered glass. "I know it sounds crazy," said my mother. "But it's true. He loved us. He wanted to be with us. And he did it the only way he knew how." She paused for a moment, and I stared at her, at the mirror. It gazed back, the glass cool and blank, as smooth and even as lake water. I walked up, stared at it, pressed my hand to the glass, as if I could reach through, touch the past. "It's not the same mirror," said my mother, gently. I shivered, imagining it: the nineteen-year-old boy, who everyone said looked a lot like my brother, lying there, in his long, green wool cloak, the stormy winds, the ice, the snow, his hands folded across his chest, slowly dying, his father in another army barracks, his mother at home with his younger sister, the dark, ice-cold hallway, the shattering of glass. "How I loved him," she murmured. "How I loved him." At night, when my parents turned out the light, I kept my eyes open, half expecting to see him there, on the other side of the room, his eyes burning in the darkness, coming back to tell us everything that he had not had been able to say.

* * *

My parents were going to the library in Giessen—my dad had some research he wanted to do—and Wolfgang and his second wife, Regina, took Adam and me boating. This is something that I never did with my academic parents, and I was wild with excitement. I loved Regina, too, so tall, so blonde, so beautiful, while I saw myself as scraggly toothed and mousy, even in braids, which I liked to imagine made me look like Laura on *Little House on the Prairie*. I wanted to imagine myself as a pioneer woman, striding across the prairie, walking in the waist-high grass, leading my horse, the covered wagon behind me, swaying in the wind. I liked that image, that independence, being where I imagined, in my childishness, that no one had been before. But here we were, now, at the river, me clutching the teddy bear that Regina had given me. Sabine, my older cousin, curled her lips and said only babies played with teddy bears. I clutched it tighter and glared at her and decided to dislike Sabine heartily. She put her long dark hair in a ponytail, stood up in her two-piece bikini, and told me that she was going for a dive off the boat and that this was something babies couldn't do. I watched her dive in, a beautiful, graceful arc, and then sat in the boat, clutching my bear, recoiling from the splashing, wondering if I could get up the courage to go in. "You need to put on a life preserver," said Regina. "Here." I held it in my lap distastefully. Sabine hadn't worn one. The water wouldn't be too cold. But Adam grabbed for the bear and it fell into the river and I lunged after it, crying, and then all I remember is the sudden swift current, the cold everywhere. I remember the reeds, floating past me, as I sank further toward the bottom, remember breaking the surface, my hands flailing, remember sinking again, remember feeling so calm, so peaceful, there near the bottom of the river, and then the arms grabbing me and gasping for air, and my brother dancing wildly on shore, flapping his arms, and Regina saying, "Your sister nearly drown and you is happy?" She shook her head. "You is a monster." I do not remember anything else.

* * *

My mother said no, he did not dance on the bank because he was happy. He did not know any better. I did not know what to say. I lay on my mother's childhood bed and only felt tired. My mother stroked my forehead, and I thought of the shattered glass and how much she had loved her brother and how much he had loved her. I did not think that I loved mine. Adam was as far away and distant from me as he could ever be. He did not want to play. When I tried to hug him, he did not hug back. I doubted that there was any way I could reach him. Then it seemed that he was happy to see me drown, but my mother said, again, no, he did not know, he did not understand. "But you know," she added, stroking my forehead again. "You understand."

I did not want to. There was, I thought, too much expected of me in trying to understand Adam, and I could feel the weight of it, as if it were a stone, dragging me under. He was the stone, the weight. I lay there in bed and thought of them, all the things I was expected to understand, and there were too many to count. I was expected to understand not having friends over, expected to understand my brother, expected to understand the war. But most of all, I thought of my brother. He seemed to be the culmination of everything, the apex where it all came together, the past and the present, in his gawky adolescent body, his blank face. I had left a war at home, and now I was hearing about war, here. I would hear bits and pieces and feel those stories sink into my body, become a part of me, a piece of my heart, a part of my vision. I could not separate myself from them, for they were a part of the air we were breathing, the food we were eating. Stories of my mother as a little girl, not too much older than I was, living in a house that was bombed. I tried to imagine that. Of the house being bombed. Of my mother, digging herself out of the rubble and running through the fields for shelter, the night sky bright with bombs exploding around the family. I could hear it in my mind as I lay in bed at night, for the house, although rebuilt brick by brick, had not forgotten the memories it was built upon. I could see her, young and tall and thin with hunger, running, her braids flying behind her, the bombs exploding, now ahead of her, now behind, looking for a home that was neither in ruin nor in flames, a family who would take them in. I could not imagine this. I could not imagine the war dead. I could not imagine the dead parents, the dead children that my mother told me of. The families who she said her mother, my grandmother, helped escape through the woods, woods we had walked through only days ago, imitating birds. I imagined them in the forest, wandering through the river, through the mud, through the snow. I imagined them in the autumn, picking the last vegetables out of my grandmother's garden, the same garden we were now enjoying, the same garden I dug into in the evening for some fresh herbs, for some lettuce. She often fed them, my mother said, stroking my forehead, the Jewish men and women she helped escape. And I imagined my grandmother, long since dead, who had insisted that my mother play with the neighborhood girls that no one else would play with because they were not Aryan children. And my mother, a child herself, faint with hunger after she had lost her home, because there was no food. And my brother, who ate and ate and ate and ate so much that sometimes I would lose my appetite, push my plate away, and say "I'm full" because I felt as if I could not eat in the face of that monumental appetite. I did not love him. He was someone whom others did not love. He was someone, perhaps, whom others would have wanted to hurt. I could understand that. I could understand wanting to hurt him. And I buried my head under my pillow. I knew I shouldn't feel like this, but there it was, buried inside me, all this darkness. At night I dreamed I ran toward it, arms outstretched, ready to push that darkness away, but despite all my running, I could never get close enough.

* * *

On the afternoon before we left, Wolfgang drove us for a boat trip down the Rhine. My mother told me the story of "Die Lorelei," the rock on which the sirens combed their hair and sang, stories of how the sirens lured men to their death by singing them beautiful songs. If they paid too much attention to them, my mother warned, everyone would drown, be sucked into the water. "Really?" I asked. I wanted to see the rock, to hear the sirens. "Ich weiss nicht, was soll es bedeuten, dass ich so traurig bin," my mother softly hummed. I know not why it is that I am so sad. The music seemed to linger in the air. I imagined the sailors catching the first strains of song, the fish-tailed women out on the rocks, their arms outstretched, waiting for their first glimpse of the seafaring men. The boat smashing into the rock. The men diving into the water after them, being lured to their deaths. I knew what that felt like. That had nearly happened to me. They would be out, charting waters that no one had seen, just as my mother must have felt on her first trip to Iowa when she had turned to my father and asked, after seeing only field upon field of corn, what must have seemed a vast expanse of silent emptiness, "Where are the people?" How, she wondered, how would she live? In a landscape so different, a culture so new. She had grown up reading myths of the American West, devouring tales of Siegfried and Walter von der Vogelweide. She loved Wagner operas as much as she deplored his ideology. She understood human contradictions. But I did not. The rock was disappointingly ordinary and gray, the music piped, the water sluggish and brown. Squat Germans sat slumped in deck chairs all around us, sipping beer, gazing nervously at the American children, fearful that any second we might start making noise. There were no sirens on rocks, combing their hair, only my brother, suddenly shrieking, a long, high-pitched wail, and his stubborn refusal to leave the boat, until my father had to nearly half-strangle him to get him off the ship, while my mother and I stood by, helplessly, wondering when, if ever, we would find any peace. And then I saw the fear on his face and felt it all over again: the pull-tug of resentment. I wished that I had the power to bridge the distance, to understand, to communicate with him. But he seemed far away, the distance to him as unbridgeable as the distance between the sky and sea.

And there would be no peace. There never could be. The waves, the water, the tides of history live there in our bodies, in all our bodies, and they never will be, never can be, washed away. I had not, after all, missed the magic moment, when we passed the rock and should have been able to hear the siren's song. It was there. It was in my brother, in his voice, high and shrill and piping, and we were not destroyed by it. We came to shore, we went home, we made dinner. We sat outside, on our lawn chairs, in the cool evening air, and my brother climbed the cherry tree in the backyard, filling the big aluminum bowl full. He filled a dish for me of the fruit; as I took it, grudgingly, still remembering that scene on the shore of him dancing, he suddenly smiled, a slow, shy, smile, and for a moment we felt like any brother and sister, sitting in the backyard, lounging in deck chairs, listening to the sounds of any summer evening. In many ways, he seemed like any brother.

And yet he is not. In his face, a face that stares off into the distance, at nothing that anyone can tell, we are free to read so much more. He is the culmination of so many things—of the waves crashing against the ship, longing to pull it under, the forced marches, all through history, of those who are different, of those we dislike, of the young men sent to their death, in Germany, in Cambodia, in Vietnam, in Korea, on and on it goes, the names, the countries, the times. Looking at him reminds us of what we are capable of: the savage cruelty but also of the undying love, those leading the persecuted to safety, those feeding the hungry, those with the capacity to forgive, the capacity to overcome, to triumph. Each day living with him is a testament to this and to human faith in the future.

I have never learned German as I would like, and sometimes I regret this, regret, now that I am an adult, that I do not know my mother's language. And then I realize that I do. That I speak that language fluently, the mother tongue. For hers was the language of survival, of resistance, the language of love, that bridged those tremendous distances between the living and the dead, between the sky and the sea, that brought her brother back home and carried mine to shore, off the boat, and into her arms. I may not speak the language of the fatherland well, the language that told her that she could not love, but I have learned to speak her own fluently, and it lives, along with history, in my body.

During the flight back home, there was a tremendous storm. My mother closed her eyes and held onto my hand; across the aisle, my father reached for her other hand while grabbing onto my brother's. "Remember," my father whispered, across the aisle, trying to get me to smile, "It's how I lost my hair." I tried to smile, although the plane shuddered and trembled and the lightning flashed. I closed my eyes and felt sick. I could hear the sirens, see the dark waters closing over me, feel the cold snows of Russia. We were far above the earth. We were floating in a sea of ice. But we were heading home. We would not forget, but we would start over again, with all that we had learned. When we made it through the dark clouds, when I felt the wheels hit the runway and heard the passengers burst into sudden, spontaneous applause, only then did I turn and open the window shade, face bathed in the sudden, blinding sunlight.

About the Authors

Catherine Anderson is the author of two collections of poetry, *The Work of Hands* (Perugia Press) and *In the Mother Tongue* (Alice James Books). Her poems and essays have appeared in the *Southern Review*, *Prairie Schooner*, the *New Virginia Review*, the *Boston Sunday Globe*, and other periodicals. She lives in Kansas City, Missouri.

Anne Clinard Barnhill is the author of two books: *What You Long For* (Main Street Rag Publisher, 2009, a short-story collection) and *At Home in the Land of Oz: Autism, My Sister and Me* (Jessica Kingsley Publishers, 2007, a memoir). Her articles and short stories have appeared in a variety of newspapers, literary anthologies, and magazines. She holds an MFA in creative writing from University of North Carolina–Wilmington.

Matthew K. Belmonte is a visiting professor at the National Brain Research Centre, Manesar, India, and brother and uncle to two people with autism. His academic background is in fiction and literature, computer science, and neuroscience—three complementary aspects of symbolic systems—and his work in these areas has been driven by the same fascination with order and regularity that motivates his brother. Belmonte's research asks what it is that makes some people in susceptible families autistic while others are spared, what are the subtle cognitive and neural traits that run in families affected by autism, and how these slight variations become converted into categorical differences.

Thomas Caramagno is the author of *The Flight of the Mind: Manic-Depression and Virginia Woolf's Art, Irreconcilable Differences? Intellectual Stalemate in the Gay Rights Debate,* and *Visible Love.* He currently teaches English at Folsom Lake College in Folsom, California.

Debra Cumberland is an associate professor of English at Winona State University in Winona, Minnesota, where she teaches creative writing and Victorian literature. She is currently the director of the Graduate Studies in English program. She has published stories, essays, and articles in several journals, including *American Literary Realism, Natural Bridge, Under the Sun,* and *The Laurel Review.* She is currently working on an edition of Willa Cather's *The Song of the Lark.*

Ann E. Damiano was an administrator and adjunct faculty member in the Division of Arts and Letters at Mount Saint Mary College in Newburgh, New York, from 1983 to 2010. Beginning in 2010, she will be the associate dean for Academic Affairs at Lebanon Valley College in Pennsylvania. Ann earned a BA in English from the State University College of New York at Buffalo, an MA in Composition Theory from the University of Buffalo, and a Doctor of Letters at Drew University. Most recently, her work has been published in *Steam Ticket 11,* a literary journal from the University of Wisconsin; the 2008 and 2009 editions of *Off to College,* a national publication for first-year college students; and *Happenings,* an alumni publication at Mount Saint Mary College. Two poems were published in the July 2010 issue of *Physiognomy in Letters.* She has written poetry, fiction (including a novel), and a memoir about growing up with an older brother with autism. Married and mother of two daughters, she is also the permanent legal guardian of her older brother, who resides in a community residence where she has served as president of the Board of Directors.

Aparna Das lives in Mussoorie, a hill town in North India. She is married to Andrew Das and has two children, Sohail and Meghna, who are thirteen and eleven years old. They live together with Anna (the youngest of Aparna's siblings) and their two dogs, Princess and Lady. Aparna is the head of the Special Needs Department of the Woodstock School, an international school in India.

Debra L. Eder is a published poet and critically acclaimed former performance artist. She lives in New York where she is currently writing a collection of stories titled "Is There Life After Debra?" and working on a memoir titled "My Brother's Speaker."

Lindsey Fisch was mentored by Dr. Bruce Mills while a psychology student at Kalamazoo College in Michigan. Knowing the sibling perspective, she worked with the special-needs community and raised autism awareness on campus. She began medical school in June 2010 and hopes to treat children with autism and related disorders someday.

Erika Reich Giles has completed certificate programs in fiction and nonfiction writing at the University of Washington. Her essays have appeared in *The Seattle Times* and other Puget Sound area publications, *Clackamas Literary Review*, *North Dakota Quarterly*, and *Ascent*. She lives with her husband on Mercer Island, Washington.

Helen McCabe is an assistant professor of education and Asian Studies at Hobart and William Smith Colleges in Geneva, New York. She is also the cofounder of The Five Project, Inc., a nonprofit organization that promotes educational, vocational, and community employment opportunities for people with disabilities in China. She has volunteered with children and adults with autism in China since 1992.

Maureen McDonnell lives and teaches in the northeastern region of the United States. Her brothers and her academic training inform her activism in disability rights, feminism, and other movements for social change.

Bruce Mills teaches at Kalamazoo College. In his field of American literature, he has authored two books (*Cultural Reformations: Lydia Maria Child and the Literature of Reform* and *Poe, Fuller, and the Mesmeric Arts: Transition States in the American Renaissance*) and has edited *Letters from New-York* (1843) by Lydia Maria Child. His creative nonfiction about his son's autism has been published in *The Georgia Review, New England Review,* and *Gravity Pulls You In: Perspectives on Parenting Children on the Autism Spectrum.* He lives in Kalamazoo, Michigan, with Mary, Sarah, and Jacob, where he continues his ongoing advocacy in relation to autism.

Erika Nanes teaches writing and rhetoric at the University of Southern California.

Katie Harrington Stricklin is a graduate of the University of Nevada, Las Vegas, and the Chapman School of Law. She is currently an attorney in Orange, California, where she resides with her husband. Katie has presented on sibling panels for national autism organizations.

Cara Murphy Watkins is working on a memoir of her brother Tim and growing up in the 1970s when little was known about autism. She has a MA in journalism and has been managing editor at weekly and daily newspapers. Her freelance work has appeared in the *Utne Reader* and *Harper's Magazine.*

Alison Wilde is a research fellow at the University of York, United Kingdom. She has interests in several areas of social care, inclusive education, and in the depiction and reception of disability and gender in a range of popular media. She has written and presented on the topics of social pedagogy, research methodology, and audience engagements with portrayals of disability in media and has published in a number of peer-reviewed journals and books. She is currently working on a longitudinal study of choice and independence in social care and continues to write and present on portrayals of disabled people on popular television and film.

Chuan (Jenny) Wu is a student at William Smith College in Geneva, New York, majoring in both Studio Art and Architecture. She and her family are from Nanjing, China.